Twayne's English Authors Series

Sylvia E. Bowman, *Editor*

INDIANA UNIVERSITY

Wilkie Collins

 94

Wilkie Collins

By WILLIAM H. MARSHALL

Twayne Publishers, Inc.   ::   New York

Preface

THIS book represents the first attempt to deal extensively and exclusively with the literary art of Wilkie Collins and the part that it played in the development of the English novel. As recently as 1932 Walter de la Mare lamented that Collins had not been included in the English Men of Letters Series, and in this he was speaking for a small but growing group of critics who had come to regard Collins as a Victorian novelist of some significance. Since that time there has been increasing attention given Collins, principally in the form of a greater number of articles in the learned and literary journals and in three biographies, the books by Kenneth Robinson (1951) and Robert Ashley (1952) and the extremely conjectural study of Nuel Pharr Davis (1956). Ashley treats widely and intelligently with critical matters, but he does so within the biographical context; thus, my own book may claim to be the first to concern itself entirely with the attributes of Collins' work. Hopefully not the last of such books, it may serve to increase our understanding of Collins' art and his place in English literature by isolating and examining, within a well-established context, certain aspects of his world and his achievement in portraying them.

My book makes two propositions. First, though Wilkie Collins was certainly a minor novelist, he was one who, clearly comprehending the dimensions and potential of the art he practiced, was able to produce major works in perhaps as many as five of his novels and to attain major qualities, however unsynthesized they might have been, in a number of other works. Secondly, as much as any, and perhaps more than most, of his contemporaries, Wilkie Collins illustrates the situation of the novelist writing during the emergence of both mass literacy and intellectual doubt: he could never abandon the claims that either the ordinary reading public or the intelligentsia had upon him; but he often failed to satisfy both and, on occasion, either of these. To comprehend the historical situation in which Wilkie Collins as a literary man found himself and what he was able to do within that situation is to understand much that is significant about the nineteenth century and its literature.

To make this book most useful to the variety of readers for whom it is intended, I have worked from the assumption that most readers have not read a number of Collins' novels. Clearly, a summary or brief description of a literary work is no esthetic substitute for the work inself, even for a work of limited literary attainment, but it may establish a basis for communication between the critic and his readers. In my chronologically ordered study of Collins' works, I have used summary or external description to the extent that any given instance seems to require it.

The question of the texts to be used is less easily resolved. Although the "library edition" of Collins' *Collected Works,* published by Chatto and Windus in the early twentieth century, seems to have the most dependable texts, the edition itself is now extremely scarce. Therefore I have turned for my quotations primarily to the seventeen-volume "library edition" brought out at various times and with continual additions between 1873 and 1893 by Harper and Brothers, Collins' American publishers. Quotations from certain of the later works not included in the Harper edition are based upon the less reliable thirty-volume edition of Collins' *Works* published by Peter Fenelon Collier in 1900; and those from the *Memoirs of the Life of William Collins, Esq., R. A.,* not included in the collected editions, come from the first edition itself.

I wish to thank Mrs. Delphine O. Richardson, of the Van Pelt Library of the University of Pennsylvania, who acquired for me various needed volumes through Interlibrary Loan. I am grateful to Mr. Alexander D. Wainwright, of the Princeton University Library, who made available to me the first editions of Collins' works in the Morris L. Parrish Collection.

The Bodley Head Limited, the publishers of Kenneth Robinson's excellent book, *Wilkie Collins: A Biography,* have graciously given me permission to quote from that work.

Mrs. Elizabeth Morrow Kist and Mr. Alan T. McKenzie, at various times enrolled in my graduate courses, made invaluable suggestions, for which I am indebted to them.

My most profound gratitude goes to Shirley E. Marshall, wife and companion, who, though she has helped me with earlier works, in the preparation of this book passed from assistant to colleague.

WILLIAM H. MARSHALL

Contents

Preface   5

Chronology   11

1. Between Two Worlds   15

2. The Early Books   27

3. The Shorter Works through 1870   40

4. The Major Novels, 1860–66   56

5. The Major Novels, 1868–70   77

6. Uneven Shadows   92

7. The World of Wilkie Collins   113

8. The Achievement of Wilkie Collins: A Conclusion   127

Notes and References   135

Selected Bibliography   143

Index   155

Chronology

1824   William Wilkie Collins born January 8 at 11 New Cavendish Street, Borough of St. Marylebone, the elder son of the painter William Collins. Sir David Wilkie stands as godfather.

1833   At this time Wilkie presumably a resident pupil at Maida Hill Academy.

1836   September, family departs for Italy.

1838   August, family returns from Italy. Wilkie attends a private school in Highbury.

1841   Wilkie apprenticed to Mr. E. Antrobus, principal partner in Antrobus & Company, a large firm of tea merchants.

1842   Summer, a journey to Scotland with his father, with a visit to Edinburgh and the Shetland Islands.

1843   August, "The Last Stagecoachman" appears in *The Illuminated Magazine*, Wilkie's first publication under his own name.

1844   August and September, Wilkie's first journey to Paris, with Charles Ward.

1846   Wilkie released by his father from Mr. Antrobus' company. May, Wilkie is entered as a law student on the rolls of Lincoln's Inn.

1847   February, the death of William Collins.

1848   The publication of Wilkie's first book, *The Memoirs of the Life of William Collins, Esq., R. A.*

1849   Wilkie in Paris, finishing *Antonina;* exhibits a landscape at the Royal Academy.

1850   *Antonina; or the Fall of Rome* published, his first novel. February, *A Court Duel* produced at Miss Kelly's Theatre. Wilkie takes a walking trip to Cornwall with Henry Brandling, as background for a travel book.

1851   *Rambles Beyond Railways*. March, Wilkie meets Dickens;

plays a part in the amateur theatrical *Not so Bad as We Seem*.

1852   *Mr. Wray's Cash Box; Basil: a Story of Modern Life*. Wilkie on tour with Dickens' Splendid Strollers.

1853   Autumn, Wilkie journeys to Switzerland and Italy with Dickens and Augustus Egg.

1854   *Hide and Seek*.

1855   June, *The Lighthouse* produced at Tavistock House.

1856   *After Dark*. November, Wilkie becomes an editor of *Household Words*. December, publication of *The Wreck of the Golden Mary*, Wilkie's first collaboration with Dickens. Early signs of physical deterioration.

1857   *The Dead Secret*. January, *The Frozen Deep* produced at Tavistock House. August, *The Lighthouse* produced at the Olympic Theatre. September, Wilkie travels with Dickens through northern England.

1858   October, *The Red Vial* produced at the Olympic Theatre.

1859   *The Queen of Hearts*. Wilkie's liaison with Caroline Elizabeth Graves.

1860   *The Woman in White*.

1862   *No Name*.

1863   *My Miscellanies*. Wilkie resigns as an editor of *All the Year Round*, successor to *Household Words*.

1866   *Armadale*. October, *The Frozen Deep* produced at the Olympic Theatre.

1867   December, *No Thoroughfare*, the last collaboration of Collins and Dickens, published in *All the Year Round;* an adaptation of it produced at the Adelphi Theatre.

1868   *The Moonstone*. January, the death of Wilkie's mother. Caroline Graves marries Joseph Charles Clow, and Wilkie's liaison with Martha Rudd, who becomes the mother of his three children, begins presumably at this time; by the early 1870's, Caroline is again living with Wilkie.

1869   March, *Black and White* produced at the Adelphi Theatre. July, Wilkie's first child, Marian, is born.

1870   *Man and Wife*.

1871   May, Wilkie's second child, Harriet Constance, is born. June, *No Name* produced at the Fifth Avenue Theatre, New York. October, *The Woman in White* produced at the Olympic Theatre.

Chronology

1872 *Poor Miss Finch.*

1873 *The New Magdalen;* also *Miss or Mrs?* and Other Stories in Outline.* February, *Man and Wife* produced at the Prince of Wales's Theatre. April, the death of Charles Collins, Wilkie's brother. May, *The New Magdalen* produced at the Olympic Theatre. Wilkie begins readings in the United States and Canada.

1874 *The Frozen Deep and Other Tales.* Wilkie returns from the United States. December, the third child, William Charles, is born.

1875 *The Law and the Lady.*

1876 *The Two Destinies.* April, *Miss Gwilt* produced at Globe Theatre.

1877 September, *The Moonstone* produced at the Olympic Theatre.

1879 *The Haunted Hotel, a Mystery of Modern Venice; to which is added My Lady's Money;* also *The Fallen Leaves—First Series.*

1880 *Jezebel's Daughter.*

1881 *The Black Robe.*

1883 *Heart and Science.* June, *Rank and Riches* produced at the Adelphi Theatre.

1884 *I Say No.*

1886 *The Evil Genius* and *The Guilty River.*

1887 *Little Novels.*

1889 *The Legacy of Cain.* September 23, Wilkie Collins dies at 82 Wimpole Street; buried at Kensal Green.

1890 *Blind Love* (completed by Walter Besant). *The Lazy Tour of Two Idle Apprentices and Other Stories* (early narratives by Collins and Dickens).

"Here is a world," said the old gentleman [Sir Patrick Lundie], getting the sun a little more broadly on his back, "which a merciful Creator has filled with lovely sights, harmonious sounds, delicious scents; and here are creatures with faculties expressly made for enjoyment of those sights, sounds, and scents—to say nothing of Love, Dinner, and Sleep, all thrown into the bargain. And these same creatures hate, starve, toss sleepless on their pillows, see nothing pleasant, hear nothing pleasant, smell nothing pleasant—cry bitter tears, say hard words, contract painful illnesses; wither, sink, age, die! What does it mean, Arnold? And how much longer is it all to go on?"

Wilkie Collins in *Man and Wife*

CHAPTER 1

Between Two Worlds

I The Writer and His Reputation

BORN in 1824 and dying in 1889, William Wilkie Collins was a significant literary figure during most of the second half of the nineteenth century. Between *Antonina,* published in 1850, and *Blind Love,* completed by Walter Besant and published posthumously in 1890, Collins wrote more than a score of novels. To these must be added the novelettes and short stories, the essays, and the plays, some of which Collins wrote in collaboration with Charles Dickens.[1] Partially trained for the law and at one point exhibiting a painting at the Royal Academy, Wilkie Collins was neither to enter the legal profession nor to follow in the work of his father, William Collins, R.A., but to devote his mature time and energies to the self-conscious and tireless creation of literature, through which his knowledge of legal matters[2] and his commitment to mimetic art continually shone and added dimension to his work.

The result of his literary work in his own time was acclaim on several occasions, infrequently matched by others during the nineteenth century. In 1860 *The Woman in White*—praised by Dickens and Thackeray as well as other writers and many reviewers—was so successful that the exploiters of public taste produced perfumes, cloaks, bonnets, and even music named after the novel.[3] Yet, in the century that opened eleven years after Collins' death, the novelist was long to hold a very small place in the critical estimate of nineteenth-century literature or even in that more spacious area, the history of nineteenth-century public taste.

In the last century, a strong personal image of a literary man frequently preceded, and on a rare occasion sustained, an intense critical concern with his work. Literary biography by some men disposed others to literary criticism. The case of Collins has been unfortunate in this respect and has adversely affected his literary reputation. Whatever the precise situation between Wilkie Collins and Caroline Graves, with whom he lived for many years, or between the novelist and Martha Rudd, who became the mother of his three children, it was obviously such that neither Collins nor those close friends familiar with the situation wished it to become part of the public domain. Thus, those who might best have written an early biography of Wilkie Collins were not disposed to do so, and for a long time those who might have been so disposed found scant data among the published recollections.

Through the years, from Collins' death to the middle of the twentieth century, the historical identity of Wilkie Collins was principally maintained by the somewhat fragmentary pictures, pleasant though they may be, given in the colorful recollections of such persons as Nat Beard and Hall Caine.[4] Only in 1951 was a full-length biography of Collins published, to be followed by two other, partially biographical books,[5] laying the foundation for additional study by those who wished to deal with Collins' writings in relation to the facts of his life. But in the path to an evaluation of Collins' literary achievement entirely on its own merit, obstacles remained, principally in the form of the way in which Collins had been classified in terms of the nineteenth-century literary situation.

Certainly, Collins was overshadowed by Charles Dickens, his friend, who was also to try—but with far greater success than Collins—to bridge the gap between the demands of serious literature and those of the mass market for books.[6] This fact lies at the heart of the ill-tempered remark, made in 1925 by Cornelius Weygandt, that Collins "is but a sort of washed-out Dickens," [7] or the more restrained comment by T. S. Eliot, one of those who rediscovered Collins and esteemed him, that "Collins . . . was a Dickens without genius." [8] John Forster, the first official biographer of Charles Dickens, possibly reflecting Forster's jealousy of Collins for which many in our century hold him guilty, minimized the association between the two novelists, casting Collins far into the shadows and giving rise to a biographical and critical literature that, whatever the intention of any of its participants, served to confirm the direction of Collins studies.[9]

In addition, much of the concern for Wilkie Collins has been at best incidental, related to his part in the development of detective fiction, expressed in histories of the *genre* or introductions to anthologies.[10] It is indisputable that *The Moonstone* (1868), one of

Collins' finest literary achievements and at the same time one of his most popular performances, is in every sense a detective story, and perhaps, for whatever significance this may give to it, the "first" in English literature. But beyond this novel there are few among Collins' works that can conceivably be called detective stories: the novel *I Say No* (1884), the novelette *My Lady's Money* (1879), and the two short stories "The Biter Bit" and "Anne Rodway." Certain of the works do contain a theme of detection, such as the novels *Hide and Seek* (1854), *The Law and the Lady* (1875), and *Jezebel's Daughter* (1880), as well as the novelette *A Plot in Private Life* (1859). But the significant point appears to be that in most of his works Collins employed the use of the rational process by one or more characters—the basis of all detective fiction—frequently juxtaposing the competing rational activities of various characters.

To regard Collins as attaining significance *only* in his contribution to the development of the detective novel is, of course, both to exclude from consideration the majority of his works and to fail to recognize how this writer, who could manipulate a number of private visions of life and action, belonged fully to the same century as Robert Browning and *The Ring and The Book* (1868–69) or George Eliot and *Middlemarch* (1871–72). That Collins did not attain their success in no way weakens the proposition that to understand his achievement, or his failure, we should turn not to categories in which he might seem momentarily to fit but to the qualities which, fully or abortively, he displays in his works.

It is not surprising, then, that relatively few critics in the last century have been concerned with Collins' work as literary art. In 1855, E. D. Forgues published an article in the *Revue des Deux Mondes* entitled "Études sur Le Roman Anglais. William Wilkie Collins," a study concerned with the early works which remains one of the most significant and appreciative.[11] Algernon Charles Swinburne's obituary essay "Wilkie Collins" revealed a very real understanding of much of what Collins had done, though in his treatment of the later novels Swinburne was perhaps too insistent upon the sacrifice of literary quality to the fulfillment of thematic intention. "But that was an evil day for his genius on which he bethought himself to try his hand at the correction of abuses, the castigation of follies, and the advocacy of reforms," Swinburne wrote, emphasizing his contention with what has become a much

quoted couplet—"What brought good Wilkie's genius nigh perdi-
tion?/Some demon whispered—'Wilkie, have a mission.'"—and
thereby establishing the basis for a critical truism in our own
time.[12]

In an essay in 1912, Arthur Compton-Rickett, though leaning
toward an "appreciation" rather than an analysis of Collins' work,
made observations that have not ceased to be useful.[13] The influence of T. S. Eliot's article of 1927 has been wide, though, in his
emphasis of what for him was Collins' most striking quality, melodrama, he might well have obscured for himself and for his readers other intrinsic literary attributes. And outstanding among the
contributions during our own generation are the articles by Robert P. Ashley and Bradford Booth, published in *Nineteenth-
Century Fiction*.[14]

From this rather limited body of criticism, supported by Collins' statements in some of his own prefaces,[15] have emerged impressions of Collins' work which, though generally sound, occasionally appear commonplace. First, there is the sense of Collins'
awareness of the demands and dimensions of his work, of his self-
consciousness as an artist, which, in the minds of some critics,
tends to suggest a devoted but ultimately mechanical manipulation of the elements with which he worked, of *talent* rather than
genius. Whatever its wellsprings, Collins' recognized awareness of
the need for plan and order in his work, persisting to the very end
of his life, is nowhere more convincingly asserted than in the Preface to *Blind Love* which Walter Besant wrote, recalling how, with
Collins' last illness, he was faced with the task of completing his
final novel:

I began by reading carefully and twice over, so as to get a grip of the
story and the novelist's intention, the part that had already appeared,
and the proofs so far as the author had gone. I then turned to the
notes. I found that these were not merely notes such as I expected—
simple indications of the plot and the development of events, but
an actual detailed scenario, in which every incident, however trivial,
was carefully laid down: there were also fragments of dialogue inserted at those places where dialogue was wanted to emphasize the
situation and make it real. I was much struck with the writer's perception of the vast importance of dialogue in making the reader seize
the scene.

The result of these detailed structural outlines has been generally recognized as Collins' superiority as a teller of tales, well summarized by Arthur Compton-Rickett under the three attributes—*"his technical dexterity as a story-teller . . . his subtle sense of dramatic effect . . . the faculty for pictorial suggestion."* [16] Nevertheless, as many of his critics have seen, Collins infrequently brings his readers into direct confrontation with violent action. There are surprisingly few instances of murder in his narratives and almost none of hand-to-hand conflict. Although his characters are on many occasions faced with the possibility of becoming trapped by their enemies and of thereafter having to find a means of physical escape, Collins rarely allows the possibility to actualize, and the reaction to the threats posed by their opponents is more often psychological than physical. Thus, Collins can become, as T. S. Eliot pointed out, the master of one aspect of melodrama, the indefinite delay, the protraction of "stage suspense"; *The Woman in White,* to use a familiar instance, is theatrical rather than truly dramatic, Eliot asserted, for it is constructed not upon "situations of conflict between significant personalities" so much as "between chessmen which merely occupy hostile positions on the board." [17]

This argument leads to the assertion that has become almost axiomatic among a number of Collins' critics—one which deserves a firmer challenge than it has received—that Collins was unable to succeed at characterization. "Even at his zenith, Collins was no reader of other men's hearts," Michael Sadleir wrote, in what is perhaps the most striking instance. "He could fashion ingenious puppets to his will, entangling them in the meshes of his intricate and faultlessly constructed plots; but neither Count Fosco nor Captain Wragge, neither Miss Gwilt nor Sergeant Cuff, remains with the reader as a new friend or as a new enemy." [18]

Such an estimate of Collins' characterizations cannot be disputed without entering the area of subjective value-response from which the estimate itself derives—a process which of course would lead nowhere. But perhaps an understanding of Collins' characters within the sociocultural context that made them even a possibility, a comprehension of the interaction of their views of life within the structure of the particular novel in which they operate, will in some instances reveal an integrity, a depth, that, subjectively, is not apparent.

Arguing against stereotypes in his essay "A Petition to the Novel-Writers," Collins asserted the individuality of character,[19] and in his work he attempted to embody the assertion. For him the absolutes of virtue and vice, by which dramatic and fictional characters had traditionally been constructed and judged, had little meaning, as he suggested through one of his spokesmen in his final novel, *Blind Love*: "Humanity, in general, is neither perfectly good nor perfectly wicked: take it as you find it." [20] Each character, so conceived and created, exists not in and of himself and his virtue or vice so much as relative to other characters and their points of view. To see him—and perhaps to value him—for what he is demands a more complex vision than merely subjective response affords, an understanding rather than an appreciation. Many of Collins' characters doubtless fail, but those that succeed do so in terms of the context in which they have been placed.

And, finally, from Collins' few critics emerges the picture of his decline as an artist during the last seventeen years or so of his life, when, ravaged by pain and ill-health and progressively addicted to the alleviating laudanum, he sank into torpid composition; he did badly those things for which he had been conditioned in the years of his creativity, when he had done them so well. In its general colors the picture is not false, and there is no possibility of disputing it. Like most generalizations, however, it loses perspective. Beginning with *Poor Miss Finch* (1872), published only four years after *The Moonstone*, the decline becomes evident. The individual character which Collins regarded as essential to good fiction generally gives way to the stereotype; intellectual or emotional simplisticism becomes attributive of a greater number of characters; plot tends to become more transparent and certainly more dependent upon coincidence and other extrinsic devices to bring it toward conclusions (poison as a means by which a character can bring on his own destruction without authorial contrivance is a factor more frequently encountered in these novels).

Yet withal, there is no steady decline, and a case can probably be made for the superiority of two novels written at the end of Collins' final decade—*The Legacy of Cain* (1889) and *Blind Love* —over several written at the beginning. Walter Besant's Preface would seem to reveal that, when unafflicted by pain and drugs, Wilkie Collins could bring to his work firm touches of what he once possessed; but he could no longer sustain this level of invention. At best, falling so unevenly upon the final novels that any generalization about them becomes slightly suspect, there are the shadows of the literary quality that once was his.

Perhaps the last novels merely accentuate what, except for the major four or five works, was Wilkie Collins' shortcoming throughout his career. If he wrote four or five major novels, he wrote more than a dozen others that, in varying ways and with little consistency, have the qualities which, synthesized in one work, produce a major novel. But in the many novels they are not synthesized, and the books themselves must remain among the minor novels of Victorian England. The cause for this failure of synthesization we cannot really determine. Obviously, it might well have been *only* the failure of Collins' ability, of the continuing capacity to bring all of his talents to a focal point.

In addition, it might have been in part his inability to meet the demands that his epoch imposed upon him. He was forced to sacrifice quality to quantity, for reasons that, though fairly apparent, lie deep in the history of the English novel. He was forced to please the broad reading public and to submit to the demands made upon the novel by its middle-class supporters (who, indeed, long continued to read Collins); he did so at the same time that he was inescapably using his art form to explore some of the questions puzzling most thinking Englishmen. Whatever qualities combine to give an author this talent for literary compromise between the two sensibilities—the intellectual and the popular—Collins possessed it only to a limited degree—and in far smaller quantities than his friends Charles Dickens and George Eliot. But this lack at least made Collins more nearly typical of the writing men of his generation.

II   *The Two Sensibilities*

The situation which Wilkie Collins faced as a novelist in the second half of the nineteenth century resulted from religious and social changes during the several centuries that preceded. The impact that the Reformation had exerted upon the literature of England must of course remain immeasurable, but certainly there were areas in which its influence was profound. To whatever degree the removal of the confessional stimulated the rise of a personal literature, such as we associate first with the Elizabethans, we cannot know; nor can we determine how much the diminution of ritual in the churches, particularly after the conjunction of Anglicanism and Puritanism, increased the intensity of the quest for esthetic gratification in literature. "In so far as the development of the Puritan tradition could, and in part did, lead to a powerful spiritualization of the personality, it was a decided benefit to literature," Max Weber, the social and economic historian, remarked. "But for the most part that benefit only accrued to later generations." [21]

The Victorians, Collins' own generation, felt the benefit (and the concomitant problems) more than any other, but the course between the Puritan reformers and the mid-nineteenth-century novelists was one marked with paradox. The reformers themselves, emphasizing private judgment, necessarily encouraged literacy in their assertions of the need that the individual therefore had for private reading; but at the same time they insisted that such reading be "true," offering men guides to their spiritual or, at least, to their practical welfare. As the Puritan ethic became secularized, resolving itself into the prudential spirit of the middle class, the belief persisted that literature should still in some way express the "true"—the practical, the provident, or the moral. Quite obviously, the stuff of novels, which themselves were born largely of the middle class, was not "true," so that far into the eighteenth century the growing middle class resisted fiction as a form of entertainment or as a means of learning.[22]

Because of the extraordinary length of a novel and the relative ease with which it could be read, it was necessary that, to flourish, the form must have an extensive body of readers, many willing to purchase large numbers each year; the prudential way of life of the rapidly expanding middle class must be somewhat eased or the novel itself must become palpably moral. Obviously, there was movement in each direction. Members of the middle class continually became more liberal, some moving steadily to orientations not associated with the class itself. But there were, through the late eighteenth and the nineteenth centuries, always new members, pushing up from the working classes into prosperity, prudentialism, and a degree of literacy. In the nineteenth century, the popular novel, resting on broad acceptance by this middle class and ostensibly exalting the virtues in which it believed, remained the constant factor.

During the first half of the century, the reader who was not wealthy faced difficulties in the procurement of books, particularly works of recent copyright, unless he could afford to subscribe to a good circulating library. Roughly from 1850 onward, however, the situation was eased for the rapidly increasing mass of readers, especially with the beginning of the practice of reprinting recent fiction and with the spread and greater availability of the circulating libraries.[23] The production of fiction seems to have matched the demand for it; in 1850 there were one hundred novels published, nearly four times as many as there had been thirty years before.[24]

One of these novels was Wilkie Collins' *Antonina*, which, though a type of historical fiction that Collins would not repeat, responded to the public demands that were in various ways to condition his novels for the next four decades. To please this public, Collins was forced to impose upon works, otherwise permeated with pathos and conceived in full awareness of the human dilemma, conclusions expressing the triumph of virtue in a simple, just, and orderly universe—conclusions that the majority of his readers believed in, though thinking men of the West had been progressively questioning them for several centuries. Although most of Collins' novels end in conventional marriages, the absurdity of the situation in which he frequently found himself might be emphasized by the endings of two of his novels, *The New Magdalen* (1873) and *The Fallen Leaves* (1879), with the hopefully happy marriage in each case of a reformed prostitute; here, responding to the extremities of his position, Collins yielded to the impulse, otherwise suppressed, to preserve the form, though not the content, of the middle-class myth.

Aside from his distrust of the shallow standards of the Victorian middle class—the pragmatic and superficial morality, the crass esthetic—which is frequently apparent though rarely made explicit in his works, Collins had grave doubts about the extent that the larger class of readers, on which the middle class itself drew for membership, had developed its capacities. In the essay "The Unknown Public," appearing in *Household Words*, Collins pointed to one of the most significant aspects of the literary scene in his own time:

The Unknown Public is, in a literary sense, hardly beginning, as yet, to learn to read. The members of it are evidently, in the mass, from no fault of theirs, still ignorant of almost every thing which is generally known and understood among readers whom circumstances have placed, socially and intellectually, in the rank above them. The mere references in "Monte Christo," "The Mysteries of Paris," and "White Lies" (the scene of this last English fiction having been laid on French ground), to foreign names, titles, manners, and customs, puzzled the Unknown Public on the threshold. Look back at the answers to correspondents, and then say, out of fifty subscribers to a penny journal, how many are likely to know, for example, that mademoiselle means miss? Besides the difficulty in appealing to the penny audience caused at the beginning by such simple obstacles as this, there was the great additional difficulty, in the case of all three of the fictions just mentioned, of accustoming untried readers to the delicacies and subtleties of literary art. An immense public has been discovered: the next thing to be done is, in a literary sense, to teach that public how to read.

*   *   *   *   *

Meanwhile, it is perhaps hardly too much to say that the future of English fiction may rest with this Unknown Public, which is now waiting to be taught the difference between a good book and a bad. It is probably a question of time only. The largest audience for periodical literature, in this age of periodicals, must obey the universal law of progress, and must, sooner or later, learn to discriminate.[25]

Once elevated to the middle class, however, a member of the "Unknown Public" was, though liberated from his own ignorance, not freed from the results of others' prejudice. In an amusing passage in his essay "A Petition to the Novel-Writers," Collins presented for his work one mode of the cultural context that was only too familiar to the Victorian novelist:

The dull people decided years and years ago, as every one knows, that novel-writing was the lowest species of literary exertion, and that novel-reading was a dangerous luxury and an utter waste of time. They gave, and still give, reasons for this opinion, which are very satisfactory to persons born without fancy or imagination, and which are utterly inconclusive to every one else. But, with reason or without it, the dull people have succeeded in affixing to our novels the stigma of being a species of contraband goods. Look, for example, at the prospectus of any librarian. The principal part of his trade of book-lending consists in the distributing of novels; and he is uniformly ashamed to own that simple fact. Sometimes, he is afraid to print the word novel at all in his lists, and smuggles in his contraband fiction under the head of Miscellaneous Literature. Sometimes, after freely offering all histories, all biographies, all voyages, all travels, he owns self-reproachfully to the fact of having novels too, but deprecatingly adds—Only the best! As if no other branch of the great tree of literature ever produced tasteless and worthless fruit! In all cases, he puts novels last on his public list of the books he distributes, though they stand first on his private list of the books he gains by. Why is he guilty of all these sins against candor? Because he is afraid of the dull people.[26]

But, to some extent, the librarian becomes Collins' scapegoat; in his own work he revealed that only with inconsistency was he himself unafraid, only on occasion and frequently with indirection did he resist the demands deriving from the "dull people" that his public placed upon his art. Had Collins consistently repudiated the shams of the Victorian middle class, for which, from the writing of *Basil* (1852) onward, he revealed such contempt, he would not have attained the popularity for which he is remembered, but he might have left a greater number of works marked by intellectual integrity and structural consistency.

Aside from his role as a successful popular novelist, Wilkie Collins was also a sensitive and intelligent man of his own times, touched by the results of the intellectual currents of the last three centuries, culminating for him in the Darwinian movement of the last years of his life. Now, no longer were all thinking men to believe as one, as indeed they had done in the Middle Ages and had attempted to do during the Enlightenment; they were no longer to argue for the reality of an ordered and just universe in which absolutes could be apprehended and defined. In the place of the reasoned faith of the earlier period and the credible reason of the more recent one, the nineteenth-century thinking man possessed as an individual only a sense of himself and his struggle for certitude, which might indeed lead him back to faith or reason (as it did for Wordsworth and Coleridge) but was based upon no public ontology, no *sense* of order that is *common* to all men.

Wilkie Collins was not primarily an intellectual, but he responded to the intellectual forces at work in his own time. His novels are filled with the quest for value, sometimes disguised in the attempt of an extremely alienated personality to find and realize his identity, sometimes presented in the conflict of individuals living in their separate selves and failing to communicate. In some instances, Collins responded to contemporary intellectual currents with what may now appear to be striking confusion, as in his attempts in *The Legacy of Cain* to deal with questions raised for him by the Darwinians. But always he remained sensitive to implications, to the quest for value—caught between the two opposing demands, the intellectual and the popular, that his epoch placed upon his art.

CHAPTER 2

The Early Books

I *Memoirs of the Life of William Collins*

WILKIE COLLINS' first published book was not a work of fiction but the *Memoirs of the Life of William Collins, Esq., R. A.* (1848). The painter, who died on February 17, 1847, some months over fifty-eight years of age, had entrusted his older son with the task of a biography, which Wilkie soon began, putting aside for the time being a work of historical fiction. Not unlike a host of other family-edited "lives and letters" that were to become a very important part of the nineteenth-century English publishing scene, the *Memoirs* is not a definitive biography but a composite of the subject drawn from a journal and an abundance of letters and the reminiscences of others. There is perhaps one difference in the *Memoirs*: the book itself offers a somewhat less personal image of the subject while it directs much attention to a detailed examination of his works as a painter.

Yet the picture of the father drawn by the son is sympathetic. William Collins was a man fully and joyously committed to a belief in the goodness of life and in the justice of its Creator; between his religion and his moving sense of the beauty of the world he found little conflict. "Go on praying to God, through Jesus Christ, to enable you, by his Holy Spirit, to be blessings to your parents; and then you must be happy," he wrote to his two sons, Wilkie and Charles, during one of his many professional absences from home. "Both your letters were well written, and I was delighted to hear you were pleased with the holiday you had on Michaelmas-day. I have made only a few sketches,—one of them, however, will, I think, please you both. It is a drawing of a large gray horse, which was brought to me from the plough" (II, 56–57). The horse itself, probably dirty from its work, was one of God's creatures, which for William Collins—as for Browning's Fra Lippo Lippi—were to be painted "Just as they are, careless of what comes of it."

Only in his strict sabbatarianism did William Collins seem to reveal a sense of cleavage between his religious belief and his commitment to life, and it is in the son's response to this aspect of the father's being that he rejected an influence which was otherwise strong upon him. Though Wilkie Collins derived from his father the firm commitment to life and beauty that marked his later activities, a devotion to his work, and a sense of its integrity as art, he clearly repudiated, at least for himself, his father's religion. The works of the novelist are filled with instances of humorless religious intensity, frequently resting upon a deception of oneself or of another; these, like the pattern of Collins' later life, may mark what his biographer Kenneth Robinson has aptly called "essentially a recoil from the somewhat austere atmosphere of his early home, and a reaction against the ascetic in the person of his father." [1]

But there is no evidence for the literal identification of William Collins with the canting Christians who appear with some frequency in his son's novels, whatever influence the father's sabbatarianism might have had on Wilkie's conception of such characters. In his reaction to his father, he obviously separated the man, who was to be esteemed, from what Wilkie himself came to consider the absurdity victimizing him. And even in his father's religion itself, Wilkie made a significant distinction between its two expressions, that which might restore the individual spirit to health and that by which one might attempt to impose his attitudes upon a group around him. In the *Memoirs*, recording the death of his father, the son ignored the latter, remarking only upon "the peaceful influences of his religion seeming to preside over his death as gently as over his life" (II, 306).

Throughout his work Wilkie Collins continued to insist upon this distinction, which became one basis for his division of the many clerical characters in his novels into the sympathetic and the deplorable. But to insist, as has been done on one occasion, that his use of the canting clergyman and the cruel father as types of character in his work expresses a hatred for his father rather than merely a rejection of his father's religion is an instance of oversimplification.[2] The *Memoirs* remains, though not a major book, a sympathetic and perceptive one; it offers significant evidence of the positive influence that William Collins was to have on his son, one to be particularly apparent in his son's work and in his sense of artistry.

II *Antonina*

Wilkie Collins' first published novel, *Antonina, or the Fall of Rome* (1850)—modeled largely upon the type of historical fiction that Edward Bulwer Lytton had been succesfully producing for nearly two decades—is undistinguished by anything except a few memorable scenes; it represents a direction in his work which Collins was not to pursue.

When the narrative opens in the year 408, Goisvintha, a wounded Gothic woman, with her deformed infant son (soon to die), has escaped from the Roman massacre of the hostages of Aquileia. Meeting her brother Hermanric, a young chieftain in the army of Alaric, Goisvintha forces from him a promise of vengeance after their arrival at Rome. Meanwhile, the sensual Vetranio, a Roman Senator, returns from pleasure-filled Ravenna to Rome, where he plans to seduce Antonina, daughter of Numerian, a religious fanatic. Shortly after Vetranio has entered the chamber of the innocent Antonina, he is surprised by Numerian, who, momentarily believing his daughter guilty, banishes her, only to recognize a moment later her innocence and regret his action. At this time the Goths, arriving at the gates of Rome, establish a blockade. In the tent of the revenge-mad Goisvintha, Hermanric promises his sister that he will slay the first Roman they encounter; Antonina, driven from her home and passing outside the walls of Rome, arrives, exhausted and nearly insensible. Goisvintha demands her life from Hermanric, who, instantly infatuated with Antonina, contrives her escape and soon establishes her in the temporary safety of an abandoned house, where he frequently visits her.

Somewhat later, the now maddened Goisvintha surprises the lovers; she mutilates Hermanric by cutting the tendons of his hands as the traditional punishment for treason, and is about to slay Antonina when the Huns arrive and, killing Hermanric, leave Antonina for dead. Finding her way to her starving father, Antonina helps him secure enough food for their survival until peace has come and Rome attains relief. Goisvintha, stalking the city for Antonina, finds and nearly destroys her enemy; she herself is murdered, as a sacrifice to a banished pagan god, by Ulpius, a displaced priest of one of the old religions, himself as mad as his victim. Found and nursed back to health by the repentant Vetranio, Antonina is installed with Numerian in a new home on the site of her supreme suffering, where hereafter she might tend the grave of Hermanric.

Ostensibly, the novel has little to recommend it. Within a complex plot, it bears characters who, in their own awareness and motivation, are strikingly simple. The theme of passing on stepping stones from one's dead self to higher things—characteristic of serious literature in the year that *In Memoriam* was published—is suggested particularly by Ulpius, the alien priest of a dead pagan god. But the theme is not developed, and Ulpius becomes, rather, a mere structural device, used to further necessary transitions though he can make none himself.

Vetranio, another character with aborted potential, undergoes a kind of moral rebirth that is neither credible nor significant. Yet the macabre scene out of which Vetranio's rebirth emerges is, for whatever sensationalist qualities it reveals, the most memorable in the novel—the banquet of famine. Expressing an absolutist reaction to the starvation facing himself and Rome, Vetranio calls to his palace other social and political leaders, who, like himself, would rather die in glorious suicide than slowly succumb to the Gothic blockade; they are to drink the wines brought forth from Vetranio's cellars until only one remains, that one to put the torch to the palace. The banquet itself reduces each guest to his moral and emotional components: self dissolves into its attributes.

To add poignance to the experience of his guests, Vetranio has reserved, for revelation at the psychologically significant moment, the shrivelled corpse of an old woman dead of starvation. An intensity unforeseen even by Vetranio is attained in the grotesquery of the moment that Reburrus, the deformed servant of Vetranio, recognizes in the apparition before them her who had been his mother. Finally, Vetranio himself is the lone survivor. As he prepares to fire the palace, Antonina enters the hall seeking food for her father. Vetranio, morally submissive to the power of her whom he once wished to submit to his own malign force, falters, and then drops the torch. If the scene which now closes has been superficially compelling, though only by the sheer horror that it attains, it renders the remainder of the novel something of an anticlimax.

III *Basil*

Basil—A Story of Modern Life (1852) represents a radical departure, in method and subject, from *Antonina*. Here, for the first time, Collins used the structural device to be exploited in many of his novels, but most adroitly in *The Woman in White* and *The Moonstone*: the accumulation and then the synthesis into meaningful narrative of the private records (letters, journals, expiational accounts, and the like) of various characters. Here also he seemed to be far more aware of the possibilities of thematic seriousness than in the first novel. "In drawing the two characters [Margaret and Mannion] whose actions bring about the darker scenes of my story, I did not forget that it was my duty, while striving to portray them naturally, to put them to good moral use," he proposed in his Letter of Dedication. "At some sacrifice . . . of dramatic effect . . . I have shown the conduct of the vile, as always, in a greater or less degree, associated with something that is selfish, contemptible, or cruel in motive." How much this kind of didactic commitment, presumably calculated to gratify a number of his readers, caused Collins to confuse his intentions in the novel and to weaken its impact, we cannot know; at least some of the implications of the narrative suggest that it is not ideally suited to the avowed moral standards of a number of its readers.

Basil, the second son of a wealthy widower, lives at home and attempts to build a literary career. He falls instantaneously in love with a linen-draper's daughter, Margaret Sherwin, a girl he has seen on an omnibus and followed to her home. Despite inevitable disgrace in the eyes of his father, Basil declares himself to Margaret's father, who agrees to an immediate secret marriage on the odd condition that Basil must wait a year to claim his wife. Accepting the situation, Basil passes his evenings trying futilely to tutor Margaret in the enjoyment of literature, against the background of her father's own dark house, where hover her mother, a woman whose goodness is rendered inarticulate by the web of evil around her, and Mannion, the mysterious clerk of Mr. Sherwin.

On the night before the expiration of the year, Basil discovers Margaret and Mannion compromised; in his rage he attacks Mannion and seriously disfigures what has been a nearly perfect face. Recovering from the brain fever that follows the shock of his discovery, Basil is disowned by his father but befriended by his sister Clara and his profligate older brother, Ralph. Margaret, visiting the hospitalized Mannion, contracts typhoid fever and dies. Mannion, horrible to behold in his recovery, vows to pursue Basil with a revenge that is without end; were it not for the intrusion of an extraneous force at a moment of crisis, when Mannion slips from the Cornish cliff and is drowned in a raging sea, he might well have succeeded. The novel ends in a way that is generally satisfactory to the sympathetic characters.

Clearly, there is a kind of operating poetic justice in *Basil*, consistent with the intentions expressed in the prefatory remarks and the demands of a middle-class reading public: Mannion, blinded in one eye, walks forth an emblem of his own moral blindness and depravity, incredibly hideous where his handsome face had once deceived; Margaret, compounding her adultery by visiting the stricken Mannion, suffers fully and obviously for her sin; Mr. Sherwin ends in bankruptcy and disgrace; Basil, whose offense against public morality is essentially imprudence, has sudden and ample cause to repent, suffering for an extended period until he is restored to that sense of order that he, at base, so much cherishes; his father, whose standards long preceded those of the middle class, is inflexible toward his son and dies in lonely age; even Ralph, the profligate rather than the prodigal son, must pay a price for the sins of his youth and become "prematurely middle-aged."

But even by offering the hardening of Ralph's tissues as a sacrifice to the avowed morality of presumed readers, Collins could not escape one of the central moral implications of his narrative, which renders it largely inconsistent with its supposed purpose. Though Basil's initial flaw might be construed as defying his father's values and wishes, once he has yielded to his love for a linen-draper's daughter, his error, bringing him into the power of the Sherwins and the sinister web that Mannion tries to build about him, lies in the honorable quality of his intentions. Had he not wished to marry Margaret but to seduce her—in effect, to follow that aristocratic ethic that Ralph himself has consistently personified—had he not sought to enter with Margaret the state which for the Victorian bourgeois was at the center of all social order—then

he would have avoided his difficulties. Like Samuel Richardson's *Pamela* (which bears the subtitle *Virtue Rewarded*) and perhaps many other instances of the middle-class myth, Collins' *Basil* must morally collapse under the weight of its own central inconsistency.

Beneath the level of explicit declaration, the novel has an aristocratic viewpoint. Ralph, for whatever price he may be paying, has a worldly sense that allows him to serve as savior to the younger brother, a fallen innocent. And the center for the nefarious activities in the novel is the house of Mr. Sherwin himself, whose fault in the eyes of Basil's father is, after all, that he is only a linen-draper; in the fact that Mr. Sherwin is committed to the exploitation of one who is attracted to his daughter Margaret, the implications are not so much that Basil's father, in his aristocratic view of life, sees wrongly as that he does not see far enough. Beneath the apparent support for the morality of the Victorian middle class in *Basil*, Collins implied strong doubt about the ultimate meaning and value of a view of life founded upon a simplistic morality and expressed through a discordant esthetic. Nothing reveals the ambiguity of the viewpoint informing *Basil*, of the conflict between the two situations facing Collins and other Victorian novelists, so much as the description of Mr. Sherwin's drawing room at North Villa:

Every thing was oppressively new. The brilliantly varnished door cracked with a report like a pistol when it was opened; the paper on the walls, with its gaudy pattern of birds, trellis-work, and flowers, in gold, red, and green, on a white ground, looked hardly dry yet; the showy window-curtains of white and sky-blue, and the still showier carpet of red and yellow, seemed as if they had come out of the shop yesterday; the round rosewood table was in a painfully high state of polish; the morocco-bound picture-books that lay on it looked as if they had never been moved or opened since they had been bought; not one leaf even of the music on the piano was dog's-eared or worn. Never was a richly furnished room more thoroughly comfortless than this—the eye ached at looking round it. There was no repose any where. The print of the queen, hanging lonely on the wall, in its heavy gilt frame, with a large crown at the top, glared on you; the paper, the curtains, the carpet glared on you; the books, the wax flowers in glass cases, the chairs in flaring chintz covers, the china plates on the door, the blue and pink glass vases and cups ranged on the chimney-piece, the over-ornamented chiffonnières, with Ton-

bridge toys and long-necked smelling-bottles on their upper shelves—all glared on you. There was no look of shadow, shelter, secrecy, or retirement in any one nook or corner of those four gaudy walls. All surrounding objects seemed startlingly near to the eye: much nearer than they really were. The room would have given a nervous man the headache before he had been in it a quarter of an hour (Part I, Chapter X).

In his prefatory remarks to *Basil,* Collins had asked, "Is not the noblest poetry of prose fiction the poetry of every-day truth?"

IV   *Hide and Seek*

In *Hide and Seek* (1854), as in *Basil,* the structure of the narrative may be insufficient for the well-developed character it contains. In that novel it is Mannion, who, though overdrawn by mimetic standards, is compelling by the sheer intensity of his sinister being; in *Hide and Seek* it is Mat Marksman. Each is a character that can be memorable without first being recognizable in terms of our own experience, one having value or meaning for us without deriving it from what we have known. And, in this novel as in *Basil,* Collins showed evidence of the difficulties of operating between two orientations, but the inconsistencies of the moral position are not nearly so apparent as before. The villain, inactive through most of the novel but nevertheless the cause of pain, is a prosperous sabbatarian, drawn from the run of middle-class Victorian life; but those who have been injured by his actions are sincere persons of various walks of life, who finally triumph by the force of the goodness that they possess which is in no way restricted to one moral code.

The novel begins with the piety of Mr. Thorpe and the long Sunday of his son Zack's childhood—as painful as anything recalled by Arthur Clennam in Dickens' *Little Dorrit* (1855–57)—and closes with the triumph of real good over false piety. In his youthful rebellion against his father, Zack is befriended by Valentine Blyth, a kind but pedestrian painter, whose aim in life is to make comfortable and happy his bedridden wife and his adopted daughter, Madonna, a deaf-mute, whose paternity is unknown. Valentine is obviously the moral center of the novel, one who, reversing the normal order in human projection, attains in *life* what he fails to attain in *art.* Madonna and, to a more restricted extent, Valentine's wife are expressions of this moral center; they

are intended, as Collins made clear in a footnote, to illustrate "with what patience and cheerfulness the heavier bodily afflictions of humanity are borne, for the most part, by those afflicted; and also . . . what elements of kindness and gentleness the spectacle of these afflictions constantly develops in the persons of the little circle by which the sufferer is surrounded" (Book I, Chapter VII).

Zack, leaving home because of his father's wrath, meets an eccentric adventurer called Matthew Marksman, who has passed much of his time in North America and has even suffered being scalped. Unknown to Zack, Mat, who has returned to England after an absence of twenty years, has learned of the seduction and death of his sister and of the existence of her child, whom he is determined to trace. The first character in a Collins novel to use rational means of detection, Mat arrives at the identity of his niece (not surprisingly, Madonna) and later of her father, Mr. Thorpe.

At the conclusion of the novel as it was first published, Mat and Zack separate in the New World, Mat going into the wilderness and Zack returning to England, where he is given an affirmative welcome by Valentine Blyth. But, as Collins candidly remarked in the Preface to the edition of 1861, after the limited success of the first edition, "guided by the light of the author's later experience," he had made revisions calculated to appeal to public taste and comfort: "I have, in one important respect, so altered the termination of the story as to make it, I hope, more satisfactory and more complete than it was in the original form." [3] Thus, in the new ending of *Hide and Seek*, "on either side, the two comrades [Zack and Mat] of former days—in years so far apart, in sympathies so close together—lived to look each other in the face again"; Mat comes to realize that the places of solitude he once loved have become strange to him, and he returns to the small group of those who care for him—those of the house of Valentine Blyth.

Whatever might be the symbolic significance of the return of the character embodying dynamic force to the moral center of the action, it was clearly undertaken for extrasymbolic reasons—for the pleasure of potential readers. Yet, *Hide and Seek* seems ultimately to be a work of more controlled and consistent viewpoint, a far more honest novel, than *Basil*. Here, though Collins, bringing the alienated Mat back to a comfort that could never be his, made concessions to the tidy moral constructs of his readers and pretended to make still others, he was able to build a work in which moral compromise, though apparent, is not destructive to the integrity of the work itself. On occasion and in but slightly veiled ways, he struck out at the drabness of the lives of those among the many potential readers demanding the moral compromise:

As for the great central portion of the suburb—or, in other words, the locality of the moderate incomes—it reflected exactly the lives of those who inhabited it, by presenting no distinctive character of its own at all.

In one part, the better order of houses imitated as pompously as they could the architectural grandeur of the mansions owned by the large incomes; in another, the worst order of houses respectably, but narrowly, escaped a general resemblance to the brick boxes of the small incomes. In some places, the "park" influences vindicated their existence superbly in the persons of isolated ladies who, not having a carriage to go out in for an airing, exhibited the next best thing, a footman to walk behind them: and so got a pedestrian airing genteelly in that way. In other places, the obtrusive spirit of the brick boxes rode about, thinly disguised, in children's carriages, drawn by nursery-maids; or fluttered aloft, delicately discernible at angles of view, in the shape of a lace pocket-handkerchief, or a fine-worked chemisette, drying modestly at home in retired corners of back gardens. Generally, however, the hostile influences of the large incomes and the small mingled together on the neutral ground of the moderate incomes; turning it into the dullest, the dreariest, the most oppressively conventional division of the whole suburb. It was just that sort of place where the thoughtful man, looking about him mournfully at the locality, and physiologically observing the inhabitants, would be prone to stop suddenly, and ask himself one plain but terrible question: "Do these people ever manage to get any real enjoyment out of their lives from one year's end to another?" (Book I, Chapter I)

If Collins was not at this stage an entirely consistent novelist as he passed between the extremes of intellectual integrity and popular appeal, he was, at least, occasionally an angry one.

V   *The Dead Secret*

The first of Collins' novels to be published in serial form, *The Dead Secret* appeared between January 3 and June 13, 1857, in *Household Words*, the periodical founded by Charles Dickens on

March 30, 1850;[4] in June 1857, it was published as a two-volume book by Bradbury and Evans. Although the very title of the weekly implied the nature of its audience, the restrictions imposed upon its writers were not rigid. Nevertheless, in *The Dead Secret* Collins was less overt in his attack upon potential readers than he had been in *Hide and Seek.* Early in the narrative he scores conformity, but the picture is general rather than restricted to the people of any class of his own day:

There is probably no better proof of the accuracy of that definition of man which describes him as an imitative animal, than is to be found in the fact that the verdict of humanity is always against any individual member of the species who presumes to differ from the rest. A man is one of a flock, and his wool must be of the general color. He must drink when the rest drink, and graze where the rest graze. Let him walk at noonday with perfect composure of countenance and decency of gait, with not the slightest appearance of vacancy in his eyes or wildness in his manner, from one end of Oxford Street to the other without his hat, and let every one of the thousands of hat-wearing people whom he passes be asked separately what they think of him, how many will abstain from deciding instantly that he is mad, on no other evidence than the evidence of his bare head? Nay, more; let him politely stop each one of those passengers, and let him explain in the plainest form of words, and in the most intelligible manner, that his head feels more easy and comfortable without a hat than with one, how many of his fellow mortals who decided that he was mad on first meeting him, will change their opinion when they part from him after hearing his explanation? In the vast majority of cases, the very explanation itself would be accepted as an excellent additional proof that the intellect of the hatless man was indisputably deranged. (Book III, Chapter I)

And at least superficially, the action conforms to the moral demands that the readers of *Household Words* might make upon it. The characters themselves are extraordinarily simplistic in their views of life, each acting in a highly predictable fashion that reveals one aspect of identity but no social roles. Each is different, serving the purposes that the plot demands for its advancement; at the same time, he is unable to deal with the emotional situations in which he is placed except by speeches which seem contrived against a general background of improbability.

In the narrative, Rosamond Treverton, born at Porthgenna

Tower, Cornwall, marries Leonard Frankland, the recently blinded son of the man who had purchased the Tower from Rosamond's father, Captain Treverton, soon after his wife's death fifteen years before. Hoping to take Captain Treverton back home after his final voyage, Rosamond, knowing that her father would never consent to return to the west rooms of the house, in use at the time of his sorrow, plans to have the unused north rooms repaired. But, when Captain Treverton dies at sea, Rosamond's hopes center on returning to Porthgenna shortly before her expected baby arrives, in order that the physician of her childhood might attend her. The baby, however, is born on the journey and later is attended by Mrs. Jazeph, a worn-out and weak-minded woman of mysterious habits and identity.

Actually, this nurse is Sarah Leeson, the one-time maid at Porthgenna Tower and the custodian of a secret letter to Captain Treverton, committed to her by Mrs. Treverton on her deathbed; Sarah, unwilling to bring pain to the Captain and his child, hid the letter in one of the abandoned rooms. And now, in a wild and ineffectual effort to save Rosamond the pain she has so long spared her, the nurse utters a warning, "Keep out of the Myrtle Room." Though Rosamond believes the strange woman insane and dismisses her, she determines to solve the mystery of the Myrtle Room as soon as she reaches Porthgenna Tower. Ultimately successful, she learns that she is not the daughter of the Trevertons or even a gentlewoman. It is this secret that Mrs. Treverton had charged Sarah to reveal to her husband; Sarah Leeson, unable to bring herself to cause pain to those she loved, fled from the house and her responsibility; then later, seeing Rosamond once more, Sarah tried to protect her by a contrivance whose transparency only her own feeble wits would fail to grasp.

Sarah Leeson is clearly at the center of the action of the novel, as Collins' readers easily saw. But she is the most significant character in the work in quite another sense; by combining certain human qualities not usually associated, she implies questions without bringing answers. In her sacrifice of herself to fulfill the charge given her by Mrs. Treverton (not to remove the letter from Porthgenna Tower) and at the same time to preserve the secret from those whose happiness it would destroy, Sarah Leeson assumes the dimensions of a truly pathetic character. But Sarah's moral commitment, altruistic in the extreme, rests upon instinct rather than free choice; she, less than any of the other major characters, is endowed with the intelligence that makes choice a meaningful reality. Sarah is, by incapacity, irrational, and the only solution to her situation, marked by crosscurrents of feeling and not by conflicting ideas, is an irrational act. But the world in which she must operate, though unable to attain moral solutions to its own problems, is at least sufficiently intelligent to recognize extreme forms of unreason and to isolate them. Alien and frightened, Sarah is driven to profound disorientation, to the verge of the insanity that the world has already attributed to her.

It is likely, however, that the majority of Collins' readers, certainly those expecting a kind of moral tidiness, missed the ironic pathos at the heart of the character of Sarah Leeson and saw instead a simple matter of personal guilt. For the physical mother of Rosamond, the woman who had given up her child that the barren Mrs. Treverton might present the baby to her husband as their own at the end of one of his long voyages, was Sarah herself. True, there was mitigation; the father, a miner named Hugh Polwheal, was killed in an accident immediately before he could fulfill the intentions toward Sarah which were honorably his. But Sarah had sinned, according to the standards avowed by the imagined readers of *Household Words*: for these readers her ultimate secret was her guilt, for which she suffered through long years. Such a reading of the novel satisfied by its moral simplicity most who came to it. That the difference in the constructions which might be put upon the title of this novel—that the secret might be the *mistress'* as well as the *maid's*—was clear to very many at the time of its popularity seems unlikely.[5] That the difference exists at all testifies to the situation which Collins encountered—that in which the meaningful novelist might both comment on the intellectual problems of his day and still present tidy moral answers for the majority of his readers—and perhaps to his ingenuity in meeting it.

The novels of Collins' early peroid contain most of the attributes found in those of the 1860's, the period of his fulfillment as a novelist. But he was still experimenting; though he was to sustain himself for ten years and through five novels, he had not yet learned to balance and integrate the demands made by the two orientations that have been discussed. The ambiguities of *The Dead Secret*, however, suggest significant progress.

CHAPTER 3

The Shorter Works through 1870

I The Novelettes

ANY discussion of Wilkie Collins' shorter fiction initially runs the risk of floundering upon the question of definition. The obvious imprecision of the terms *novelette* and *short story* is compounded by the fact that, whatever the first form of publication might have been (often in *Household Words* or *All the Year Round*), a number of the shorter pieces of fiction were indiscriminantly collected as "stories" in *After Dark* (1856) and in *The Queen of Hearts* (1859). In general, the division employed in this study, between the novelettes and the short stories, has been set forth by those previously concerned with Collins and his work; though it is not always borne out by significant differences in lengths.

Qualitatively, the differences may be even less discernible. So long as Collins restricted himself to an incident or at most a brief episode, as in "A Terribly Strange Bed," success in the short story was likely. But to protract the narrative to a series of events or to attain the *sursis indefini* supporting certain kinds of dramatic effect, he required greater length than the short story allowed. Most of his novelettes are well constructed and filled with characters of credible and significant motivation, but the novel offered the opportunity most suited to Collins' abilities. Aside from the restrictions placed upon him by ill health and by his work as an editorial associate during the early years of *All the Year Round* (established by Dickens on April 30, 1859),[1] there may be other significance in the fact that during his major period—from the appearance of *The Woman in White* in 1860 through the publication of *Man and Wife* in 1870—Collins published neither novelettes nor short stories; certainly, the amount of work required to create the five major novels is a principal cause, but the degree to which they satisfied his creative demands remains at least a possibility.

Mr. Wray's Cash Box, Collins' first novelette, was published in one volume by Bentley as a Christmas book in December, 1851. A work of slight intrinsic merit, it came between *Antonina* and *Basil;* it marks, therefore, Collins' departure from the model set forth by Bulwer Lytton to the "actual." Although the influence of Dickens (and particularly of the Dickens of Christmas stories and plum pudding) is easily discernible, certain subjects and techniques which become familiar in Collins' later fiction are apparent here: the lack of action and mobility, the use of dreams, the concern with shock and alternating psychological states, types such as the country squire and the parson, and art used as a symbol of identity.

Mr. Reuben Wray, in *Mr. Wray's Cash Box,* a retired player of small parts under John Kemble, makes a living for his granddaughter Annie by giving elocution lessons and by directing amateur private theatricals (all in the manner of the adored Kemble). At Stratford-on-Avon, Reuben secretly takes a mold and makes a cast of the famous Shakespeare bust; afraid of discovery, he quickly leaves Stratford and goes to Tidbury-on-the-Marsh, with the mask in his otherwise empty cash box. Chummy Dick and Benjamin Grimes steal Reuben's box, expectedly believing that it contains cash; in the course of their flight, they shatter the mask and with it Reuben Wray's symbol of identity. The old man falls into shock and hovers near insanity. Annie, knowing that the mold was left at Stratford, returns secretly, and retrieves it. Thereafter, repressing all recent recollections by accepting their content as a dream, Reuben is able to join his granddaughter and his Tidbury friends for a huge and jolly Christmas dinner.

Gabriel's Marriage (1853) reveals a significant improvement in the control of materials and the penetration of a character's state of mind. Set in Brittany during the suppression of the Church by the French Revolution, the story concerns a young man's suspicions that his father has committed murder, which he regards as a moral barrier to his own planned marriage. Only after Gabriel has seen his simple world shattered by these suspicions, which are themselves ultimately resolved, can he begin to build a new kind of faith—one sustained by the image of Father Paul, the messianic priest who defies the Revolution—and then to look forward to happiness with his betrothed, Perrine. Although the theme of expiation, to become central in much of Collins' later work, has been implicit in Numerian's guilt over misjudgment of Antonina and in Basil's writing the story of his terrible error, it is first made explicit in the task that Gabriel's father assumes in payment for his crime: rebuilding wayside crosses destroyed during the Revolution.

Sister Rose (1855), a tale of the French Terror, involves the sentencing of the innocent and the momentary triumph of the guilty. It sustains suspense until the dénouement; yet, by dividing the story into parts, between which action can be assumed to occur and time to pass, Collins was able to avoid the direct report of action that in this case would have detracted from the state of psychological tension through which the narrative survives. The structure of the novelette rests upon the principle of duplexity, the struggle of wits between the treacherous former aristocrat, Charles Danville—who betrays his brother-in-law and his wife to the Terror—and Lomaque, once the land-steward for Danville and now an official of the Revolution. Lomaque finally wins, of course; while, in a memorable scene, Danville is exposed as the hypocrite that he is. Because of the intensity of the action and mood, the relief that the conclusion brings—with death for Danville and secluded peace for Rose—far outweighs any incredulity felt about the means by which Lomaque saves the lives of Rose Danville and her brother during the resultant confusion as Robespierre goes to the guillotine.

That Rose is saved marks an emerging characteristic of Collins' work, which, for better or worse, was to be exploited in a number of ways—the return to life of those presumed by someone to be dead. In Collins' first novel Antonina herself was left for dead by the Huns and later stabbed almost fatally by Goisvintha; in *Basil*, Mannion recovers from the beating which the protagonist fears has been fatal; the grandfather of young Gabriel makes a deathbed confession and glides into the darkening shadows, but before they have become opaque, he momentarily emerges to retract his words; and in the same narrative the victim of "murder" rises to walk again. In each instance revival is essential for the furtherance of the narrative beyond a specific point; in *Sister Rose* the return to life and freedom of those presumed to have died becomes the central point on which all action and the resolution of the narrative must rest.

In *The Yellow Mask* (1855)—a work firmly in the Protestant middle-class tradition, akin to Matthew Gregory Lewis' novel *The*

Monk (1796)—Father Rocco, a Pisan priest and the brother of the master-sculptor Luca Lomi, schemes that Luca's daughter Maddalena might marry Fabio, a wealthy nobleman studying under Luca. Having learned that Fabio's family acquired much of its wealth during the confiscation of Church lands, Rocco hopes by his scheme to restore what he feels rightfully belongs to the Church. But Fabio falls in love with Nanina, a poor young girl modelling in the studio, whom Father Rocco subsequently persuades to disappear to Florence, where he places her in a family that can spy on her for him. Fabio marries Maddalena, who dies in childbirth, leaving a daughter, whom Rocco must now plan to train in order to influence Fabio to restore the Church's wealth.

Nanina, discovering that Father Rocco has arranged to have her watched, quietly returns to Pisa, where she obtains work serving at a masked ball at which, it is rumored, Fabio will make his first social appearance following the death of his wife. At the ball, Fabio is persistently annoyed by a woman in a yellow mask, who, finally alone with him, removes the mask and reveals what appears to be the face of his wife. In the shock that follows, Fabio hangs near death but is slowly nursed to health by Nanina. By accident, she discovers that the woman was Brigida, once hopeful of marrying Fabio and acquiring his wealth, who has been in the employ of Father Rocco; hoping to frighten Fabio and thereby prevent his marriage to Nanina, Rocco had taken a mask of Maddalena from a statue in Luca's studio. Discovered, Rocco makes a confession to Rome; he is soon summoned there and is heard of no more. Brigida leaves Pisa, "alone and penniless." And, completing the moral tidiness of the conclusion, Fabio and Nanina find happiness, rearing Fabio's daughter by his first marriage.

Collins wrote *Mad Monkton* in February 1852, but—first rejected by Dickens, on the grounds that its subject, hereditary insanity, might distress the readers of *Household Words*[2]—it was not published until late in 1855 in *Fraser's Magazine*. The narrative concerns one episode, recalled in a straightforward fashion by the speaker, a friend to Alfred (sometimes called "Mad") Monkton; its effects depend largely upon language and situations calculated to protract uncertainty and to intensify suspense:

> At the head of the staircase my friend the *attaché* met me.
> "What! going away already?" said he.

"Yes; and on a very curious expedition. I am going to Monkton's rooms, by his own invitation."

"You don't mean it! Upon my honor, you're a bold fellow to trust yourself alone with 'Mad Monkton' when the moon is at the full."

"He is ill, poor fellow. Besides, I don't think him half as mad as you do."

"We won't dispute about that; but mark my words, he has not asked you to go where no visitor has ever been admitted before without a special purpose. I predict that you will see or hear something to-night which you will remember for the rest of your life."

We parted. When I knocked at the court-yard gate of the house where Monkton lived, my friend's last words on the palace staircase recurred to me, and, though I had laughed at him when he spoke them, I began to suspect even then that his prediction would be fulfilled. (Chapter II)

As it turns out, Alfred Monkton is not at all dangerous. The survivor of an ancient Roman Catholic family, he is presumed to carry the family curse of insanity, to which others attribute any unusual behavior on his part. Actually, it is quite a different curse that Monkton feels himself bearing; for this reason he has postponed his marriage and made the present journey to Naples. An ancient family prophecy, written on the blank leaf of one of the manuscripts at Wincot Abbey, foretells that at the time one of the Monktons lies unburied under a foreign sky, "Monkton's race shall pass away." Alfred Monkton wishes, therefore, to locate the resting place of his scapegrace uncle, Stephen Monkton, reportedly killed in a duel, and seeks the narrator's help in his search.

Slowly, guided by the rational conclusions on the part of the narrator, they move closer to the location of the body. The narrator approaches a monastery, of which the description, equalling anything else in Collins' work, illustrates one way that Collins, using a single episode, sustained interest in his narratives. It begins:

It was a dark, low, sinister-looking place. Not a sign of life or movement was visible any where about it. Green stains streaked the once white façade of the chapel in all directions. Moss clustered thick in every crevice of the heavy scowling wall that surrounded the convent. Long lank weeds grew out of the fissures of roof and parapet, and, drooping far downward, waved wearily in and out of the barred dormitory windows. The very cross opposite the entrance-gate, with a shocking life-sized figure in wood nailed to it, was so beset at the base with crawling creatures, and looked so slimy, green, and rotten all the way up, that I absolutely shrank from it. (Chapter V)

The speaker proceeds, however, and discovers the body of the slain Monkton, unburied and rotting in an outbuilding of the monastery. In time, after various kinds of negotiation, Alfred Monkton prepares to return with the body to the vaults of Wincot Abbey. He thus believes that, if the curse someday is worked out effectively, it at least will not do so through his agency or neglect. But the body remains *outside* the vaults of the Abbey, and the prophecy *is* fulfilled. The storm that sinks the boat is not in any way extrarational, a fact that is of some structural significance; the narrative itself, cast in the words of a highly rational speaker, is primarily concerned with the natural means by which an essentially supernatural prediction is fulfilled.

The Dream Woman (1855), a straightforward story, has some of the qualities of the ballad narrative. An ostler, "Unlucky Isaac" Scatchard, spending a night away from home in an inn, is attacked with a knife by a "dream woman," who is fair and fine and has a slight droop in her left eyelid. In the years that follow this incident, he encounters the woman of the dream once more, marries her in sympathy, but discovers her to be a drunkard who indeed attempts to murder him with the same knife. The preoccupation with the apparition and what it foretells for the protagonist is an early instance of Collins' use of the prophetic dream, a device appearing with increasing frequency in his later works. Here, as in the novel *Armadale* (1866), a character gives a full account of a dream, in this instance Isaac to his mother, that she might record it as a warning against events of the future.

As in most of Collins' other works, two sensibilities are operating in *The Dream Woman.* By one, that of Isaac Scatchard and his mother, the dream is regarded as at least supernaturally revelational, a prophecy; by the other, ironically informing the narrative from a point outside it, recording the events in the episode, the association between dream and reality is seen as coincidental but in no way necessary. The presence of the two sensibilities is far less obvious than in *Mad Monkton,* in which the tone of the narrative is explicitly rational. As in the case of determining the real nature of Sarah Leeson's "dead secret," the reader is allowed a choice of what to believe; and by his choice he does not judge the story so much as the story reveals *his* sensibility.

A Rogue's Life (*Household Words,* 1856; 1879) represents a departure from Collins' characteristic mode. In the manner of Thackeray's *The Memoirs of Barry Lyndon Esq.* (1884), the outlaw tells his own story, thereby passing significant judgment upon the society that has superficially judged him. Thus, the work becomes the first full instance of Collins' fiction of social purpose, though here it is cast in a facetious tone that on occasion may seem overbearing. Collins did not return to this type of fiction, in which an outlaw is sympathetically portrayed as the central character. However, in *No Name* (1862) Captain Wragge dominates much of the action, accumulating sympathy for his roguery as he continues to act. As in much picaresque storytelling, the rogue himself is extraordinarily likeable.

The son of a physician who is kept poor because he must live up to his own position as son-in-law to a Lady, the narrator of *A Rogue's Life* is soon forced to earn his way in the world by his own devices. These always assume the form of fraud—copying "Old Masters," which are then sold as authentic; serving as secretary to a Literary and Scientific Institution in the town of Duskydale; and finally, counterfeiting coins. In each case, by his deception of society he judges the very people who through their laws would claim to judge him. Ultimately, of course, he must triumph, for the society in which he operates is essentially false and will in time find a place for a man of consummate fraudulence.

In Australia, to which he has been transported, he is able, by the adroitness of his maneuvers, to become, two years before the expiration of his sentence, "a convict aristocrat—a prosperous, wealthy, highly respectable mercantile man. . . . I have a barouche and two bay horses, a coachman and a page in neat liveries, three charming children, and a French governess, a boudoir and lady's-maid for my wife. She is as handsome as ever, but getting a little fat. So am I, as a worthy friend remarked when I recently appeared holding the plate, at our last charity sermon" (Postscript). Presumably, a prosperous reader of *Household Words* would be amused at the narrator's evil doings or at the chase of the counterfeiters by the Bow Street Runners; he would see not himself in the concluding portrait but a rather dreadful fellow who had managed to prosper in Australia, where the laws were not very firm and where society was not founded on sound business principles.

The final novelette during this period, *A Plot in Private Life* (1858), offers little in comparison with its predecessors. It concerns the marriage of a wealthy widow to an enterprising man, Mr. James Smith, who soon becomes his wife's foil, just as Josephine, an unfaithful maid to Mrs. Smith, becomes the foil to Mrs. Smith's faithful servant and confidant, William. Despite Smith's attempts at extortion, his bigamy, and Josephine's having Mrs. Smith and William prosecuted for Smith's murder, the principal villain is found to be living—in that kind of revival that Collins often used—and all ends well.

Clearly, during this period Collins' attainments in the novelette were as uneven as his subjects were varied.

II *The Short Stories*

Aside from the short stories in the Christmas numbers of *Household Words,* in which Collins collaborated with Dickens to an undetermined extent, before 1860 Wilkie Collins wrote and published ten short stories. Of these, the most celebrated among Collins' shorter pieces and the one most frequently anthologized is "A Terribly Strange Bed" (1852). In it, two young Englishmen in Paris decide to visit a blackguard gambling house, where the narrator breaks the bank at *rouge et noir.* Made drunk in celebration by those who own the house and persuaded to pass the night, the narrator soon realizes that he has been drugged; fighting his impulse to sleep, he finally lies down but becomes aware, barely in time, that the top of the canopy of the bed is descending to crush him. In the narrative there is little conflict, except between the narrator himself and the forces of evil which momentarily he is unable to explain. As he learns later, the canopy is controlled not by any force beyond comprehension but by a simple mechanism operated through the ceiling from the room above. The effect of this story derives from the sustained tension created by the struggle between the man and the unknown force.

In "The Stolen Letter" (1854), a trivial piece, the son of a haughty squire, about to marry a governess, is victimized by a blackmailer; when he is saved by a benign lawyer—a familiar Collins type—the story ends on a happy note. More successful is "The Lady of Glenwith Grange," written especially for

publication in *After Dark*. Suggesting Miss Havisham of Dickens'
later novel *Great Expectations* (1859), Ida Welwyn, a spinster,
retains Glenwith Grange as a macabre monument to her own
dead past and to the younger sister whose tragic marriage had
destroyed her. The story has sufficient incident, credibly recorded,
to sustain it.

"The Diary of Anne Rodway" (1856) is both Collins' first use of
the epistolary method—to become one of his most important devices—and his first murder mystery. Anne, a miserably poor
young woman, supports herself by needlework. Her close friend
Mary Mallinson, the daughter of a brutal drunkard and a woman
even more desperate than Anne, is an addict to laudanum. One
night Mary is brought home unconscious from a blow on the
head, from which she dies. Though the inquest rules her death
accidental, Anne refuses to accept this verdict; tracing the murderer by a clue found on Mary's person, Anne solves the crime.

"The Siege of the Black Cottage" (1857) is an undistinguished
recounting of a young girl's bravery in saving a sum of money
belonging to others from the grasp of two petty outlaws. "Uncle
George; or the Family Mystery" (1857) concerns a young man's
discovery of the reason for the disappearance of a favorite uncle
many years before. "The Dead Hand" (1857) is, perhaps more
than any other of the short stories, an incident deprived of external conflict. The story rests upon the protagonist's opposing responses to the situation in which he finds himself when he shares a
room with twin beds in an inn with a person whom he soon presumes to be dead.

In Collins' "The Biter Bit" (1858), usually regarded as the first
humorous detective story,[3] Matthew Sharpin, a somewhat too
confident young man who is forced by others upon the Detective
Police, is given his first case; he incredibly mismanages it with what
amounts to a travesty of the rational process. The absurdity of his
activities in the fulfillment of his role is intensified by the epistolary form that the story assumes, with the majority of the letters
coming immodestly but revealingly from Sharpin himself. "I am
now comfortably established next door to Mr. Jay, and I am delighted to say that I have two holes in the partition instead of
one," Sharpin writes, characteristically, to Chief Inspector Theak-
stone of the suspect he is pursuing:

My natural sense of humor has led me into the pardonable extrava-
gance of giving them both appropriate names. One I call my peep-
hole, and the other my pipe-hole. The name of the first explains itself;
the name of the second refers to a small tin pipe or tube inserted in
the hole, and twisted so that the mouth of it comes close to my ear
while I am standing at my post of observation. Thus, while I am looking at Mr. Jay through my peep-hole, I can hear every word that may
be spoken in his room through my pipe-hole.

If "The Biter Bit" is the most amusing of this group of stories,
"Fauntleroy" (1858) is clearly the warmest. Based upon the life
and death of Henry Fauntleroy (1785–1824), hanged for
forgery,[4] the story is told by one man who, though recognizing
fully the evil in Fauntleroy's act, nevertheless defends him as a
man with strong loyalties and personal integrity. Like so many of
Wilkie Collins' other characters, the protagonist emerges as one
who is tempered in his worst moments by a strong flame of good.

Following "Fauntleroy," "The Parson's Scruple" (1859) comes
as an anticlimax. In this story a fundamentalist preacher who
marries a young "widow" discovers that she is really a divorcée,
and leaves her. Represented is an early form of Collins' protest
against the unfairness of marriage laws in the United Kingdom.

The majority of Collins' short stories, while not outright failures, probably have little to recommend them either on esthetic
grounds or for the needs of the modern reader. Of the ten published before 1860, "A Terribly Strange Bed" might be joined in
the anthologies by "The Dead Hand," "The Biter Bit," and
"Fauntleroy," each bringing to the collection its own particular
appeal. But, beyond these, each of the others probably best serves
the student of literature in revealing an analogue with a major
element in one of Dickens' principal novels or in displaying the
growth in Collins' own work.

In 1856 Collins brought together three of his novelettes and
three short stories in the two volumes which Smith and Elder published as *After Dark*. He made some attempt at imposing cohesiveness upon the collection by casting it as a volume dictated to
Mrs. Leah Kerby by her husband, a travelling portrait painter
whose ailing eyes force him to rest from his accustomed work and
to find another means to support his family—the production of a
collection of the stories that he has heard during his professional
travels.

In 1859, when Hurst and Blackett published his second collection, *The Queen of Hearts*, Collins was more persuasive in the frame that he imposed upon the work. Three old brothers who have retired to their ancient house, the Glen Tower, are, by the terms of an oddly conceived will, paid a visit of six weeks by a young girl named Jessie Yelverton. In order to amuse her, and to prolong her stay until the son of one of the old men can arrive at Glen Tower to propose to her, the old men conceive the idea of telling stories, each drawn from the experiences of one of them, during the evenings near the end of her visit. Though the framing narrative hardly maintains suspense about the outcome—whether the young man will arrive in time and succeed in winning the girl—it establishes a cohesive background in mood that derives from the setting of the marvelous old house itself and from Collins' exploitation of the varying potential that the weather offers.

III   The Plays

In the Letter of Dedication prefixed to *Basil*, Collins remarked that "the Novel and the Play are twin-sisters in the family of Fiction; that the one is a drama narrated, as the other is a drama acted; and that all the strong and deep emotions which the Playwriter is privileged to excite, the Novel-writer is privileged to excite also." A number of his novels obviously use dramatic (or even theatrical) techniques. Collins was interested in the theater; if he was less successful as a playwright than as a novelist, the causes may lie in the way in which, for the most part, he derived his plays from his novels and stories—instead of working in the opposite direction—and in the manner in which his plays were composed: occasionally the result of collaboration, they were at best somewhat makeshift, usually adapted to the changing needs of those presenting them and therefore not assuming a permanent form until they had passed from the living theater.

There were, in the years before 1860, only four plays with which Collins was connected. *A Court Duel*, which Collins translated from an unidentified French original, was performed in three acts at Miss Kelly's Theatre in Soho on February 26, 1850, with Collins himself in the lead. *The Lighthouse*, his adaptation in two acts of the novelette *Gabriel's Marriage*,[5] was first produced at Dickens' residence, Tavistock House, on June 16, 1855, then publicly at the Olympic Theatre in August 1857. *The Frozen*

Deep, which—despite his usual procedure—Collins was later to turn into prose (1874), was originally a drama in three acts conceived by Collins and Dickens, though written largely by Collins, which was produced at Tavistock House on January 6, 1857, and then at the Olympic Theatre nine years later. *The Red Vial*, also in three acts, from which Collins was to write one of his more lively novels of the last years, *Jezebel's Daughter* (1880), was produced at the Royal Olympic Theatre on October 11, 1858.

Later, in the 1860's, Wilkie Collins was in some way related to five plays, though not always as sole author. "A Message from the Sea," a story on which Collins and Dickens collaborated for the Christmas number of *All the Year Round* in 1860, was adapted to the stage and apparently presented for four weeks in early 1861 at the Britannia Saloon, Hoxton. However, neither Collins nor Dickens seems to have been responsible for this adaptation; indeed, they heavily protested against the performance, threatening legal action and writing to *The Times*. Somewhat later that year, presumably with the intention of protecting their dramatic copyright, they arranged to have *All the Year Round* publish their own synopsis of the plot to be used in a dramatic version; but their play seems never to have been written.[6]

In two instances during the 1860's, Collins made stage adaptations of his own novels. In 1863, in collaboration with W. B. Bernard, he wrote a dramatic version of *No Name*, published by the office of *All the Year Round*, which was followed in 1870 by his own privately printed version. Collins was never satisfied with his adaptations of this novel, and it therefore did not reach the boards. His friend, Wybert Reeve made an adaptation that so pleased Collins that he encouraged Reeve to produce the play, as he did in Australia and perhaps in the United States.[7] Late in 1866 Collins was at work upon an adaptation of *Armadale*, which had recently appeared both in serial and volume form. This play was never produced, though a vastly different version by Collins, entitled *Miss Gwilt*, reached the stage in 1875. François Joseph Régnier, of the Théatre Français, a friend of both Collins and Dickens, made an adaptation of *Armadale* in his own language, but there is no certainty that it was performed.[8]

For the Christmas number of *All the Year Round* in 1867, Collins and Dickens wrote "No Thoroughfare," a short story which, slightly after its original composition, Collins himself adapted to the stage. Beginning at the Adelphi Theatre on December 26, with Charles Fechter in the lead, the play ran for two hundred nights—the longest run of any of Collins' dramas. In the United States, the situation did not turn out so happily for the authors; despite the fact that Dickens, then on tour in America, registered the play in the name of his Boston publishers, Ticknor and Fields, first one, then many, of the theaters produced their own versions of the drama.[9] Late in the next year, Collins worked with Fechter to produce *Black and White*, a drama about the racial situation in Trinidad that opened at the Adelphi on March 29, 1869. With Fechter in the lead, the play ran for six weeks before a brief provincial tour and, in 1871, production in Boston.[10]

IV   *The Essays*

In the years preceding 1860, Wilkie Collins wrote and published approximately four dozen essays, nearly all of them appearing in *Household Words* and its successor *All the Year Round*. From this great number of essays might be drawn but a handful possessing significant literary merit. The essays which Collins contributed to *All the Year Round* between January, 1860, and July, 1865, probably reveal somewhat greater literary value because they reflect the fulfillment of his abilities apparent in the novels of the 1860's. They do not, however, significantly differ in subject and type from their predecessors.

In 1863, possibly at the time that Collins resigned as editorial associate of *All the Year Round*, he selected, from the essays that had appeared in Dickens' two periodicals, a number that seemed worthy of reprinting. In October of that year, somewhat revised, these were published by Sampson Low as *My Miscellanies*. In his Preface to the collection, Collins recalled what his intentions had been in writing the essays now collected: "My object . . . was to present what I had observed and what I had thought, in the lightest and least pretentious form; to address the public . . . with something of the ease of letter-writing and something of the familiarity of friendly talk."

In general, Collins admirably fulfilled his intentions, achieving in the essays, for whatever literary merit they might lack, a familiarity and lightness of tone. He was occasionally swept into seriousness by the very subject with which he was treating, more likely than not when he was acting as the social or literary critic. But, by restricting his subjects to the pleasantly personal or to those areas of life which he could view with detachment or satiric irony, he was usually able to avoid the danger.

There are, in the body of Collins' essays, expectedly, some reminiscences, such as the somewhat facetious essay "My Black Mirror," his recollections in "Laid Up in Lodgings" of life in Paris and London during two of his rheumatic attacks, or the biographical sketch of a beloved friend (one of the few essays that are appropriately serious), "Douglas Jerrold." [11] More frequently, however, Collins used a persona in order to maintain the detachment so necessary to the levity of tone. The old bachelor who speaks in "My Spinsters" or in "Bold Words by a Bachelor" is one with whom Collins, at thirty-two, was not yet ready to identify. Perhaps somewhat closer to the author himself is the speaker in "Save Me From My Friends," who, seeing a mendicant appealing for money because "he has no friends," thinks of his own friends who disturb him and ruin his work. In "A Shy Scheme," a man claiming to be so shy that he cannot propose marriage wishes for a *Handbook of Courtship* written by British ladies, who might thereby instruct him in the proper language; to this Collins wrote a reply, "Awful Warning to Bachelors," in which the speaker recalls how the book *Etiquette of Courtship and Marriage*, sent to him as he was about to become engaged, persuaded him to remain single. In the satirical essay "Sure to be Healthy, Wealthy and Wise," the speaker is a man who pretends to believe in the advertisements he reads. And in "Pray Employ Major Namby!" the speaker is a spinster who complains of a particular habit of her next-door neighbor.

The image of the obnoxious Major Namby, imposed upon the reader's vision by the persona that the author has assumed, has the stuff of fiction as much as of the essay, revealing how often in this body of work the distinction between *genres* collapses. In "Mrs. Badgery," the situation may be more obvious, if only because the character of whom the speaker complains may appear as somewhat more overpowering. "Mrs. Bullwinkle" is a nurse who, employed to care for the speaker's new baby, is rapidly eating more than the speaker can afford to supply. In the first piece that Collins published under his own name, "The Last Stagecoachman" (1843), the identity as an essay is almost totally obscured by the speaker's recalling a dream-vision in which, at a deserted wayside inn once a center of the stagecoach business, he meets the last stagecoachman, a man whose spirit has been bent but not broken by the coming of the railroad. In similar fashion, "A Sermon for Sepoys" contains an oriental tale calculated to teach that the expression of life most acceptable to the Supreme Being is a life that is most useful to the human race.

The several essays concerned with crime which had first appeared in *All the Year Round* and were then collected in *My Miscellanies* as "Cases Worth Looking At"—"The Poisoned Meal," "Memoirs of an Adopted Son," and "The Caldron of Oil"—preserve their *genre* only by Collins' claim made in a footnote that "the facts of each narrative exist in print, . . . [though] the scarce and curious books from which my materials are derived have been long since out of print, and are, in all human probability, never likely to be published again" (*My Miscellanies*, p. 215).[12]

In other instances Collins more or less wrote as himself, though inevitably the subjects and forms which he imposed upon his essays tended to limit him in each instance to a role or persona. Taken together, many of these pieces present a body of miscellaneous social observation that never really becomes social criticism. The concern of "Talk-Stoppers" is fairly obvious. "A Journey in Search of Nothing" deals with those modern beings who attempt, in leaving the city and its noises, to find peace and rest in the country, but discover that they have really exchanged old distractions for new without really solving their problems. "Sea Breezes with a London Smack" develops a different aspect of the same situation: seeking to escape from the city with all its modern horrors, a man discovers that London's civilization has extended to the seaside itself. "New View of Society" is an amusing attack upon the absurdity of wearing the uncomfortable clothes of civilization, especially in the heat of midsummer. "An Unreported Speech" is a forceful objection to the music that is imposed upon unwilling ears in public places, a piece with significant implications about the conflict of taste between the crass majority and the sensitive minority in Victorian England.

The essays that somewhat more closely approach social criticism are generally of greater seriousness and are occasionally marked by a note of anger. In the essay "Highly Proper!" Collins attacked the prejudice that many Englishmen felt against actors and their families. "Strike!"—a somewhat more facetious piece—concerns the passivity of the middle class to some of the ridiculously unpleasant conditions of modern life. And "A Breach of British Privilege" points to the absurdities of excessive patriotism and dependence upon the public ritual of the nation. In at least one case, "The Unknown Public," Collins' social criticism, here perhaps not quite so light as the Preface to *My Miscellanies* would make it appear to be, has amply served later social historians.

This essay has critical implications, a fact that is hardly surprising. Yet, in the body of Collins' essays published during the 1850's and 1860's, there are disappointingly few concerned with literature, and of these not all are really critical. "A Petition to the Novel-Writers," Collins' organized objection to the stereotypes still found in fiction, remains useful. "Dramatic Grub Street. Explored in Two Letters" sets up the problem in the first letter, from "Mr. Reader," to be answered in the second, from "Mr. Author": essentially, since the London theater lacks quality, the solution is to encourage (as the French have long done) those who write other works of quality to regard the drama as a significant literary outlet. "A Fair Penitent" is more nearly characteristic of Collins' writings upon literature; in this instance he describes two manuscripts among the papers of Charles Pineau Duclos. "A Dramatic Author" is a review of Edward Fitzball's autobiography,[13] and "Portrait of an Author, Painted by his Publisher" is a vastly interesting and well-written sketch about the life of Balzac.

On other occasions Collins played the historian, writing in "A Remarkable Revolution" of Elizabeth Petrovna's assumption of the Imperial throne of Russia; in "A Queen's Revenge," of a particular incident in the remarkable career of Queen Christina of Sweden; and in "A Great (Forgotten) Invasion," of an abortive French foray into England in 1797. As elsewhere, judged from the viewpoint of Collins' limited aims, the essays are satisfactory, but they hardly express the fulfillment of his ability.

CHAPTER 4

The Major Novels, 1860–66

I *The Woman in White*

*T*HE *Woman in White* appeared serially in *All the Year Round* between November 26, 1859, and August 25, 1860; like some of Collins' other novels, it was published in *Harper's Weekly,* where it concluded three weeks earlier.[1] In August, 1860, it was published in book form by Sampson Low in England and by Harper and Brothers in the United States. The impact of the novel upon the public could be measured by the continuing rise in the circulation of Dickens' weekly and by the sales of the book itself, which a rival publisher was later to describe, with but slight exaggeration, as "the most popular novel of the century." [2] In this novel Collins was able for the first time to attain close to full synthesis between the qualities demanded by artistic integrity and by his readers.

The story of Laura Fairlie's forced marriage to Sir Percival Glyde, of the secret concerning Sir Percival which involves the mysterious Anne Catherick, of Laura's incarceration as a person and later her forced eclipse as a personality—the massive Count Fosco casting a darkening shadow of evil over all the action with only the colorless Walter Hartright left, finally, to oppose him—is more well known. In a preface which Collins wrote for a later edition, he remarks that "the primary object of a work of fiction should be to tell a story"; he also emphasized that "It may be possible, in novel-writing, to present characters successfully without telling a story; but it is not possible to tell a story successfully without presenting characters: their existence, as recognizable realities, being the sole condition on which the story can be effectively told." In *The Woman in White* there is a vast array of characters, far greater than in the earlier novels. However Count Fosco may strain initial credulity, he remains the most memorable of all these characters, according to the critical consensus of the last hundred years. Suggesting a refinement of the Gothic villain, Fosco is.

really a type of character new to the English novel; his learning is as extensive as his person and his ego, his white mice run playfully along his strong arms, and his suave irony bespeaks inward control. His power as a character derives from that same uncomfortable literary condition from which springs Satan's in *Paradise Lost,* or even Becky Sharp's in *Vanity Fair,* especially when they are cast against Adam or Amelia: the propulsion on which narrative or dramatic literature depends derives from a conflict between forces, which cannot spring from good alone. In this sense, only evil is dramatic and the colorful Fosco, unique as a personality, relentlessly spreads, like evil itself, over the action.

Set in opposition to Fosco, initially fascinated though fearful and distrusting, is Laura's half-sister, Marian Halcombe. "I certainly never saw a man, in all my experience, whom I should be so sorry to have for an enemy. Is this because I like him, or because I am afraid of him?" Marian writes in her diary not long after Count Fosco's arrival at Blackwater Park. She is aware of his power over her, as apparently over every living creature—a power achieved in each case by the most carefully calculated means: "I know he flatters my vanity, when I think of him up here, in my own room—and yet, when I go down stairs, and get into his company again, he will blind me again, and I shall be flattered again, just as if I had never found him out at all! He can manage me as he manages his wife and Laura, as he managed the blood-hound in the stable-yard, as he manages Sir Percival himself, every hour in the day" (Second Epoch. Marian's Diary, II).

Part of the meaning of all experience lies in the resolution of the confusion of appearance and reality. Marian has already sent away Laura's suitor, Walter Hartright, and her own and Laura's drawing-master, so that Laura's marriage to Sir Percival Glyde can proceed without impediment; only in time, as the opposition between Fosco and herself assumes moral tones, does she recognize her error. Only at the end of their struggle—when Marian lies ill, and Fosco is able to read her diary and thus to conquer her with the power over another being that is born of knowledge—does Walter Hartright return to the conflict with Fosco and Glyde, appearing now in full heroic stature, to fill the moral vacuum created by Marian's defeat.

T. S. Eliot, perhaps excessively sensitive to the enormous moral conflict in *The Woman in White,* remarked that Fosco and Marian alone sustain the dramatic structure of the novel.[4] Despite this observation, there are in *The Woman in White* other characters of significant dramatic quality. An instance is Mrs. Eliza Michelson, the widowed housekeeper at Blackwater Park, who contributes a short narrative to the collection, constituting the history of the struggle between the beings of good and Count Fosco. Unaware of the direction of the action that she recounts, Mrs. Michelson belies what she says of her own tolerance by the way she expresses it and by the very fact that she feels compelled to talk of it at all: "I have always cultivated a feeling of humane indulgence for foreigners. They do not possess our blessings and advantages, and they are, for the most part, brought up in the blind errors of popery. It has also always been my precept and practice, as it was my dear husband's precept and practice before me (see Sermon xxix., in the Collection by the late Rev. Samuel Michelson, M.A.), to do as I would be done by."

Thus, deceived by Fosco's appearance in his entreaties, unable to attain even a partial understanding of the meaning of her experience, Mrs. Michelson attributes Laura's dislike of Fosco to prejudice, remarking, "I never before met with any lady of her rank and station who was so lamentably narrow-minded on the subject of foreigners." In the end, without a sense of her own inconsistency, Mrs. Michelson exculpates Fosco, but blames his instrument in evil, Mrs. Rubelle, as "that foreign person" (The Story continued by Eliza Michelson). More aware of the construction she has put upon her experience, Mrs. Catherick, addressing Walter Hartright, stands forth in ironic perspective, in which may be one of the most striking of the overlooked dramatic monologues in nineteenth-century literature:

"You don't know how I have lived in this place, and what I have done in this place, Mr. What's-your-name," she went on. "I'll tell you, before I ring the bell and have you shown out. I came here a wronged woman. I came here robbed of my character, and determined to claim it back. I've been years and years about it—and I *have* claimed it back. I have matched the respectable people fairly and openly, on their own ground. If they say any thing against me now, they must say it in secret: they can't say it, they daren't say it, openly. I stand high enough in this town to be out of your reach. *The clergyman bows to me.* Aha! you didn't bargain for that, when you came here. Go to the church, and inquire about me—you will find Mrs. Catherick has her sitting, like the rest of them, and pays the rent on the day it's due. Go to the town-hall. There's a petition lying there; a petition of the respectable inhabitants against allowing a Circus to come and perform here and corrupt our morals: yes! OUR morals. I signed that petition this morning. Go to the book-seller's shop. The clergyman's Wednesday evening Lectures on Justification by Faith are publishing there by subscription—I'm down on the list. The doctor's wife only put a shilling in the plate at our last charity sermon—I put half a crown. Mr. Church-warden Soward held the plate, and bowed to me. Ten years ago he told Pigrum the chemist I ought to be whipped out of the town at the cart's tail. Is your mother alive? Has she got a better Bible on her table than I have got on mine? Does she stand better with her trades-people than I do with mine? Has she always lived within her income? I have always lived within mine.—Ah! there *is* the clergyman coming along the square. Look, Mr. What's-your-name —look, if you please!" (Third Epoch. The Story continued by Walter Hartright, Chapter VIII)

The quality most apparent in the brief parts played by these and a number of other minor characters in *The Woman in White* is dramatic irony. A literary device which developed with rapidity during the nineteenth century, dramatic irony particularly marks Collins' characterizations in a number of his novels; it is attained in great measure through the structural method associated with him by which each person tells his story as it appears to him. With the breakdown of the single standard of value unifying Medieval man and informing his literature, the individual was thrown back, in his quest for value, first upon reason, then upon himself and his own experiences. The difficulty of the quest began to emerge as a dominant concern of literature, and, after several centuries, with the collapse of the Enlightenment, the individual's evaluation of his own experiences came in literary works to be set within a larger context, constituting a more comprehensive orientation that rather clearly revealed the limits of his own perspective.

With the juxtaposition of the two orientations, dramatic irony became a viable literary possibility, marking not only the poetry of Lord Byron and Robert Browning but of many of the other poets and novelists. Using the conventional materials of the novel, such as letters and journals, and caught between the intellectual and popular Victorian orientation, Wilkie Collins was well situated to develop the narrative potential that dramatic irony offered him. In most of these instances, the narrative consists of the records of characters who participated in or witnessed the action which have been brought together and edited, either by the protagonist or by someone relatively detached from the central action but sufficiently wise to impose meaning upon it.

In *The Woman in White*, it is Walter Hartright who collects and arranges these records. In doing so, he fully exploits the principle illustrated by the results of Fosco's reading of Marian's diary during her severe illness: that knowledge leads to power. For this structural method to succeed as a means of dramatic development, in the juxtaposition of any two characters one must know more than the other and be able to utilize what he gains from the other's unknowing revelations; with equal knowledge or with identical orientations of two related characters, all action or development would cease. Revelation itself is thereby continually active, and knowledge becomes a form of motion. In visiting Mr. Frederick Fairlie for a brief interview, Count Fosco, possessing the power given him by the reading of Marian's diary, can easily control Fairlie; while pretending to give Fairlie knowledge, he actually moves to the certitude that his own plans will work. Reduced merely to the totality of his own symptoms, Mr. Fairlie similarly reduces Fosco and all other men to the totality of their own apparent attitudes; for Fosco, on the other hand, Fairlie attains reality only at the moment of active revelation, when what knowledge he possesses becomes motion.

Comprehending all individual revelations and possessing all significant knowledge, from which comes his very power to be what he is, Walter Hartright as editor of the documents juxtaposes time present, with its total awareness, and time past, with only the knowledge that one situated in a particular position at that time could possibly have. Thus, for example, Walter can impose his footnotes and other editorial apparatus upon his materials; he can exploit the full dramatic potential of juxtaposing even more than two levels of awareness. When, as an instance, Marian Halcombe records in her diary her early impressions of Count Fosco, she unsuspectingly comments upon his apparent relations with his countrymen; later, reading her diary, Hartright moves closer to an understanding of the true situation of Fosco, a knowledge giving him the power to defeat Fosco, which only now, at the time of his editing the documents, can he put into the full perspective that the present affords him. He is able to see the part

played by the various minor characters in the episode with which
he is concerned; his friend Pesca, appearing at the beginning and
end of the episode, for example, seems to envelope the action
without having any part in it; through him, Hartright first meets
the Fairlies and finally triumphs over a deeply frightened Fosco.

There are several types of document which Hartright uses. Narratives of the past such as Mrs. Michelson's assume a fixed dimension, a static reality, confined to the past, and they thereby fall
short of truth. A narrative such as Marian's diary is somewhat
different, for it is a nearly contemporary record of events, in
which the writer cannot know at any given time what she may
later learn and ultimately provide her narrative with the perspective that it now lacks. Marian's diary is an instrument by which,
moment-by-moment, she can order reality to her liking; once lost
from her control, however, it becomes the means by which another can attain power over her.

And there is also the kind of document represented by the letter
that, long ago, the mother of Marian Halcombe and Laura Fairlie
wrote about the young Anne Catherick, recording impressions
made well before the central events of the episode, which attain
perspective only at the time that Walter Hartright imposes order
as he edits the record of Marian's reading of the letter itself.
Within the larger circle of Hartright's present awareness are many
smaller circles, the narratives and records of others, some of them
concentric. By the control that he attains in his narrative method,
Walter Hartright, explicitly casting the reader in the role of judge,
offers him an object with which he can make an intellectual identification.

In quite another way Hartright becomes the object of identity,
in the struggle against evil: he triumphs over casuistry and stud-
ied complexity with an honest rationalism and an amiable simplicity that the reader feign would recognize as his own. In the second phase of events, Count Fosco proposes what is essentially his
view of man's life and action. "The machinery that it [society] has
set up for the detection of crime is miserably ineffective—and yet
only invent a moral epigram, saying that it works well, and you
blind every body to its blunders from that moment," he remarks
to the company at Blackwater Park. "When the criminal is a brutal, ignorant fool, the police, in nine cases out of ten, win. When
the criminal is a resolute, educated, highly-intelligent man, the

police, in nine cases out of ten, lose. If the police win, you generally hear all about it. If the police lose, you generally hear nothing."

Fosco's position seems to be not *immoral* so much as *amoral;* it
essentially denies rather than opposes the reality of good. For
Fosco, virtue is without substance because it is without function
in society, and society for him constitutes the only significant form
of the universe. He operates therefore not in a universe where
good and evil struggle but where there is no moral dimension:

"English society, Miss Halcombe, is as often the accomplice, as it is
the enemy, of crime. Yes! yes! Crime is in this country what crime is
in other countries—a good friend to a man and to those about him
as often as it is an enemy. A great rascal provides for his wife and
family. The worse he is, the more he makes them the objects for your
sympathy. He often provides, also, for himself. A profligate spend-
thrift who is always borrowing money, will get more from his friends
than the rigidly honest man who only borrows of them once, under
pressure of the direst want. In the one case, the friends will not be at
all surprised, and they will give. In the other case, they will be very
much surprised, and they will hesitate. Is the prison that Mr. Scoun-
drel lives in, at the end of his career, a more uncomfortable place than
the work-house that Mr. Honesty lives in, at the end of *his* career?
When John-Howard-Philanthropist wants to relieve misery, he goes
to find it in prisons, where crime is wretched—not in huts and hovels,
where virtue is wretched too. . . . Which gets on best, do you think,
of two poor starving dress-makers—the woman who resists temptation, and is honest, or the woman who falls under temptation, and
steals? You all know that the stealing is the making of that second
woman's fortune—it advertises her from length to breadth of good-
humored, charitable England—and she is relieved, as the breaker of
a commandment, when she would have been left to starve, as the
keeper of it." (Second Epoch. The Story continued by Marian Halcombe, Chapter III)

One of the most significant utterances in the novel, it transforms
Fosco from a colorful stock villain into a character of total self-
awareness. It imposes upon Hartright, as Fosco's principal opponent after the fall of Marian, both the defeat of Fosco (which is
indeed accomplished for him by others) and the demonstration,
by the display of his own superior powers of reason and sympathy, of the weakness in Fosco's position.

For this reason, physical action in *The Woman in White* is neither significant nor obtrusive. Knowledge rather than strength remains always the basis for power, and the physical forces that literally destroy first Glyde and then Fosco have no relation to the intellectual forces rallied by Walter Hartright. The relation between Sir Percival Glyde and Count Fosco is important, for within the structure of the novel they serve quite different functions, each clarified by the other. Glyde, once described by T. S. Eliot as "a figure of pasteboard," [5] can actually have no more than the physical dimensions of which Eliot complained; he is a form of reactive villainy, as much exploited by Fosco himself as he is by the circumstances of his life; he is a man almost totally externalized in his responses. Glyde commits deeds of evil in his own person or through his servants acting at the physical level.

And here lies, of course, the essential difference between Glyde and Fosco. The course of evil that Fosco pursues operates through the mind rather than the body; its power is derived from Fosco's knowledge of men and of the reasons that they trust him. Thus, doing as he wills them to do, they fall ultimately into the delusion that they are acting in full autonomy; thinking that they identify his will with their own, they thereby reduce theirs to an aspect of his. For Fosco, the life of what some men deem evil has been refined to a rational exercise that is to be exulted in and enjoyed.

It is hardly surprising that Glyde falls before Fosco does. Hartright's encounter with the English baronet simply prepares him for the finer contact that is to follow. Significantly, though Hartright and Sir Percival have long been juxtaposed, especially since the one loves the wife of the other, their meeting is postponed until after Glyde's death, when the physical forces that represented the limits of his comprehension have done their work. Like Glyde, Fosco has been to Walter Hartright personally unknown; until shortly before their encounter, the enormous nobleman has been a creature of Walter's mind, imaged and conceived, the sum of his attributes. Here the resemblance ends between Walter's encounters with the minor and the major villains.

His meeting with Fosco is marked by nothing approaching physical violence, for even the pistol that Fosco clutches in the drawer of the table beside him is rendered useless by the superior power of Hartright's knowledge and reason; the triumph is complete only when Fosco writes his own Narrative, in an act mark-

ing the subordination of his will *and of his reason* to those of
another; Fosco has been beaten in the only terms that in his life
have constituted reality. His identity has been, in effect, destroyed; what power remains, merely reflective, must now pour
into the Narrative he writes, art reflecting life; in a marvelous moment of fallen splendor, he sets forth, another Satan on his burn-
ing lake.

Walter Hartright is an instrument of truth rather than, in any
punitive sense, of justice. The punishment of Fosco, by standards
understood and imposed by the world of men, is left to other
hands. Hartright's accomplishment is far more significant than
this. Using the terms of success, even of survival, that Fosco himself established in his amoral pronouncement at Blackwater Park,
Hartright now refutes the substance of Fosco's pronouncement:
there is a good, Walter Hartright demonstrates, and it *works*.
With this moral position, which had sustained the English middle
class through several centuries, the majority of readers of *The
Woman in White* would consciously concur. Perhaps, in one sense
if in no other, Count Fosco and Hartright would agree: in the
judgments that they imposed upon the activity of the mind, both
were ultimately pragmatists. Even in his sophisticaton and complexity, Count Fosco was the kind of villain that many of Collins'
readers would feel they understood.

What, then, of Walter Hartright? He stands triumphant before
Fosco, but, in the flamboyant writing of his own recollections,
Fosco steals the scene. The encounter may resemble what we
might imagine—what any true-born Englishman of the middle of
Victoria's reign might have imagined—of Adam's quiet triumph
over Satan after Eve had but temporarily strayed, had the Fall
never really occurred and had *Paradise Lost* never been written as
it was. In other words, Hartright's victory, seen in one context,
represents the total defeat of evil by the forces of good in a world
in which all men would like to believe. But perhaps Hartright's
defeat of Fosco seemed to many Victorian readers to resemble
nothing so much as Miss Pross' victory over Madame Defarge in
Dickens' *A Tale of Two Cities* (1859), the triumph of quiet English virtue over flamboyant foreign vice.

For, as colorless as Adam himself, Walter Hartright is, above
all, the one character in *The Woman in White* with whom the true-
born Englishman of Collins' day, represented in the mass of

middle-class readers, could identify. "You know the character which is given to my countryman by the English?" Fosco asks Marian Halcombe. "We Italians are all wily and suspicious by nature, in the estimation of the good John Bull" (Second Epoch. Marian's Narrative, IV). At this point, he proceeds to argue, as he demonstrates later, that he is not unlike the image of his countrymen attributed to the minds of the English. Ironically, the popularity of the novel may give some support to the conjecture that vast numbers of Englishmen held the stereotype of which Fosco accused them. For, despite the use of Hartright's Italian friend Pesca as an instrument of redemption, evil—in a superficial view of the novel—would still be associated with the foreign in the person of Fosco and good with the English in the person of Hartright.

This is not to propose that Collins himself held any such notions of national virtue; in a number of areas he far preferred the Continental to the English ways. Rather, caught between the demands of esthetic or intellectual integrity and public taste, he had learned—and in the character of Walter Hartright illustrated—how these might be fused. Hartright becomes the structural center of the novel and, despite a certain degree of dramatic irony, the character through whom the intellectual implications are brought together and explored.

On the other side, quiet but sturdy, he embodies most of the qualities and the virtues with which the middle-class readers would associate themselves. The son of a thrifty drawing-master, he is set against a nobleman and a baronet; he is continually frustrated by a decadent member of the gentry in Frederick Fairlie. Whereas Fairlie dabbles in art, Hartright takes it with all due seriousness, working at it as any *good* man would work at his occupation. In his struggle first for recognition in his profession and then against seemingly insurmountable odds for the happiness of the one he loves, Hartright works hard and displays reason, courage, and endurance—all the virtues of the Puritan ethic, by which the middle class lived and survived. He is providential in his thinking, and he is committed to the belief, cheerfully avowed, that ultimately all works for the fulfillment of good. Yet he is tolerant, even of those who do evil: "The best men are not consistent in good—why should the worst men be consistent in evil?" (Third Epoch. Hartright's Narrative [Second Part], II). In the end Walter Hartright is rewarded for the good work he has done, not only by his marriage to Laura but by the birth of a son, who becomes thereby the "heir of Limmeridge."

II *No Name*

While, in the early novels, there were intimations of social protest, and in *The Woman in White* the arranged marriage of Laura Fairlie and the emergent social position of Sir Percival Glyde implicitly bespeak social protest, Collins fully assumed his role as social critic in *No Name* (1862). He was primarily concerned with the injustice of the marriage laws and with the difficulties that resulted from them, especially in matters of inheritance. The "marriage" of Mr. and Mrs. Andrew Vanstone—the parents of Magdalen, the female protagonist—is far more real in its relation to human value and attainment, though it lacks sanction of the Church or the law, than the legal marriage which Magdalen herself makes with Noel Vanstone—one undertaken through hatred and contrivance on one side, stupidity and deception on the other.

Clearly, the more obvious implications appealed to the reason and good sense of the middle class constituting the majority of Collins' readers. The anti-bourgeois inference was probably not drawn by them from the fact that, had Mr. Andrew Vanstone in his youth—like Basil in the earlier novel—exploited but not married the young adventuress, he would have brought no problems in his middle years to himself and to his children. Similarly, the suggestion would pass unheeded by most readers that the comically villainous Captain Wragge is simply an instance of laissez-faire taken to extremes. For Wragge himself proposes: "Do you think me mercenary—I merely understand the age I live in" (Last Scene, Chapter II).

But Collins was unwilling or unprepared, in his criticism of specific social abuses, to make a too obvious attack upon the very value-structure sustaining the majority of his readers. Instead, drawing implicitly although not explicitly upon the Christian tradition of Magdalen with its various implications, Collins created a myth concerning the possibility of morality and cast it in the modern waste land, which on occasion he overtly described:

The net-work of dismal streets stretching over the surrounding neighborhood contains a population for the most part of the poorer order.

In the thoroughfares where shops abound, the sordid struggle with poverty shows itself unreservedly on the filthy pavement; gathers its forces through the week; and, strengthening to a tumult on Saturday night, sees the Sunday morning dawn in murky gas-light. Miserable women, whose faces never smile, haunt the butchers' shops in such London localities as these, with relics of the men's wages saved from the public-house clutched fast in their hands, with eyes that devour the meat they dare not buy, with eager fingers that touch it covetously, as the fingers of their richer sisters touch a precious stone. In this district, as in other districts remote from the wealthy quarters of the metropolis, the hideous London vagabond—with the filth of the street outmatched in his speech, with the mud of the street outdirtied in his clothes—lounges, lowering and brutal, at the street corner and the gin-shop door; the public disgrace of his country, the unheeded warning of social troubles that are yet to come. Here, the loud self-assertion of Modern Progress—which has reformed so much in manners, and altered so little in men—meets the flat contradiction that scatters its pretensions to the winds. Here, while the national prosperity feasts, like another Belshazzar, on the spectacle of its own magnificence, is the Writing on the Wall, which warns the monarch, Money, that his glory is weighed in the balance, and his power found wanting. (Scene III, Chapter I)

Wealth and poverty, each implying the other, are the contrasting coordinates of the moral background. In dividing *No Name* into eight "Scenes" rather than books or parts, with groups of letters and other documents constituting the sections called "Between the Scenes," Collins emphasized the picaresque elements in the novel, but the setting is more than simply geographic. In creating the myth of Magdalen Vanstone's moral journey, he gave *No Name* a significant degree of intellectual integrity without sacrificing its popular appeal.

In general, the action conforms to Collins' description of it in the Preface to the first edition: "The only Secret contained in this book is revealed midway in the first volume. From that point, all the main events of the story are purposely foreshadowed, before they take place—my present design being to rouse the reader's interest in following the train of circumstances by which these foreseen events are brought about." Most of the action in the narrative springs from the schemes that Magdalen conceives for the recovery of the fortune that she regards as rightfully belonging to her and her older sister. Norah, the sister, accepts her situation;

though she comes in time by a marriage of love again into the
fortune, she consciously does nothing to re-establish her inheritance.

Magdalen, moved by a sense of rectitude that ironically contains the seeds of her own moral destruction, contrives with the
aid of art (disguise and impersonation) and of Captain Wragge
to marry her cousin, the pitiable if contemptible semi-invalid Noel
Vanstone (son of her father's already wealthy brother Michael, to
whom the fortune reverted) and thereby to regain what she thinks
is hers. Her legitimacy she cannot hope to retrieve: since her
father had foolishly married in his youth, he and Magdalen's
mother were able to legitimatize their union only after the death
of his first wife. But, before he could complete a new will, providing for his grown daughters, both he and his wife died, leaving the
girls without legitimate claims to his name or his fortune.

That Magdalen is concerned with only the lost fortune is, of
course, an expression of her realistic response to worldly affairs,
but it also limits the context in which she is to operate. After her
disappearance from the stricken home, she encounters Captain
Wragge, a distant relative of her mother, a man who is moved by
the idea of retrieving the fortune but has no concern for any kind
of legitimacy; he becomes thereafter Magdalen's tutor in duplic-
ity, first on the stage and then in life, and the measure of her loss
of moral orientation. Despite her marriage to Noel Vanstone and
his subsequent death, Magdalen's schemes are ultimately unre-
warded; after an intense period of moral alienation, however, she
is reclaimed from both physical illness and the sense of her own
degradation by her marriage to Captain Kirke.

To the point of the collapse of Magdalen's hopes, the narrative
is sustained by the duel of wits between the English Captain
Wragge and the French Mrs. Lecount, the housekeeper and sustaining force of the sickly Noel Vanstone, whose claim to villainy
must rest on *how* she responds moment-by-moment to situations
rather than on the larger grounds of her fulfilling what is clearly
her responsibility to Noel Vanstone. Since she no more than
Wragge is concerned with moral considerations in attaining her
ends, there are no restrictions upon the devices each uses to abort
the schemes of the other. At the end of the action, having lost
contact with Magdalen and Wragge at the time of Noel Vanstone's death, Mrs. Lecount fades into the life of the Continent,

while Captain Wragge becomes prosperous as the seller of patent medicines, thereby socially mitigating what villainy has not already been absorbed by the increasingly comic aspect of his being. Neither is punished, for more than any of their villainous predecessors, Captain Wragge and Mrs. Lecount illustrate Collins' view of the relativity of evil, the mixed nature of virtue and vice.

In large measure the case is such because the moral struggle takes place not in the outer world, between men and women competing for that world's rewards, but in the being of Magdalen Vanstone. "Magdalen! It was a strange name to have given her?" asks the narrator. "Strange, indeed; and yet, chosen under no extraordinary circumstances. The name had been borne by one of Mr. Vanstone's sisters, who had died in early youth" (First Scene, Chapter I). Yet, Magdalen develops to fit the name; her story becomes a myth about the possibility for fall and redemption in the modern world. The implications of the myth are, so far as Magdalen's story must inevitably relate to the lives of others, somewhat ambiguous; and the resolution imposed upon the conclusion of the narrative, by which Magdalen is redeemed through her spontaneous love for Captain Kirke ("church"), a savior come from the sea, is at best somewhat contrived.

Viewed mythically, the Vanstone girls' disinheritance is essentially that of modern man. Betrayed by the past, whose safeguards of their security have proved inadequate, Magdalen and Norah become "Nobody's Children" and are left by the law "helpless at their uncle's mercy." That Magdalen soon brings herself to repeat these words (First Scene, Chapters I & II) and that Norah does not reveals that the difference between them is one of emotional assimilation and of intellectual response as well as of particular temperament. In her reaction to their common state, each of the girls represents an opposed ethic, a view of life. Though Norah may sustain herself by what she feels is inner strength—an indifference to what the world may give or take away—Magdalen can find in Norah's forbearance only the evidence of weakness.

The differences, seen in one light, concern their relative distinctions between one's *identity* (what one essentially is) and one's various *roles* (aspects of identity evident in one's relation to society). For Norah, identity seems to be a quality developed within, so that to be a "Vanstone" and to inherit money would be merely to fill a role. For Magdalen, identity is defined by what one possesses; disinheritance means a loss of selfhood. The comprehensive viewpoint of the novel, the "meaning" of the myth, is explicitly on the side of Norah, and is supposedly made clear when she in her meekness retrieves her inheritance. Ultimately, however, Norah does so only because Magdalen, having in her humility learned the lesson of Norah's truth, destroys in a final gesture of expiation the Trust which, it is discovered at a late moment, would cause half of the estate of Noel Vanstone to revert to Magdalen as his widow.

However the meaning of Magdalen's story may fail to relate to other persons in a social context, in itself it illustrates the moral deterioration that follows the individual's attempts to impose meaning and order upon his own existence, irrespective of the impact upon those with whom he is associated. The question implied, though not pursued, is whether modern man, forced to total self-dependence—without the aid of whatever the past once bestowed upon him—can survive in both the moral and the economic realms of his being. In the case of Captain Wragge and elsewhere, Collins approached the question; but—he never fully asked it, and certainly he never answered it.

Magdalen Vanstone, whose first name has been explicitly, but not implicitly, deprived of any intended significance, discovers that she has had no claim to the surname and the fortune that it represents, both symbols of an accustomed social identity. In her attempt to retrieve this identity, she increasingly subordinates means to ends and loses her moral identity; in effect, she falls. Thus, though the name "Vanstone" no longer belongs to her, the name "Magdalen" accumulates significance for the reader from the early part of the traditional Christian story. As an actress, working under the guidance of Captain Wragge, Magdalen begins the rapid assumption of roles which is to mark her quest for identity but ironically to remain what Captain Wragge literally calls it, "a triumph in the art of self-disguise" (Third Scene, Chapter II). At length, with ritualistic overtones, she directs Wragge "to dispose (as privately as possible) of every article of costume used in the dramatic Entertainment. I have done with our performances forever; and I wish to be set free from every thing which might accidentally connect me with them in the future" (Between the Scenes [third and fourth], XI).

Abandoning the necessary theatrical distinction between appearance and reality, Magdalen hereafter assumes disguises (the marks of roles) only in life. She has now moved completely from the innocent world of Combe Raven, her childhood home, to the world of Captain Wragge, marked by the Captain's wife, who sits stupidly in essential disorder as the sole means of an occasional contact with morality—"the only innocent creature in this guilty house." When Magdalen sells herself in the loveless marriage to Noel Vanstone, she confirms the inner significance that has been accumulating about her first name, and she retrieves no more than the form of what was once her last name. Only at the conclusion, in the repentance sustained by the pressure of Captain Kirke, does Magdalen attain full moral identity and become significantly part of what the tradition of her namesake means.

Again, Collins' readers, if they did not directly blame him for the creation of a heroine with moral ambiguities, would find little sustaining value in the myth itself. Nor would they have seen its weaknesses and inconsistencies; Magdalen, for example, in the hour of her redemption, largely uses upon Kirke the devices for persuasion that she has practiced upon others during the time of her fall. They would rarely have recognized the essential fact about Kirke's power as Magdalen responds to it: that it derives from his capacity to be unlike, to be larger than, those constituting the public itself. " 'Do I deserve my happiness?' she murmured, asking the one question at last. 'Oh, I know how the poor narrow people who have never felt and never suffered would answer me if I asked them what I ask you. If *they* knew my story, they would forget all the provocation, and only remember the offense; they would fasten on my sin, and pass all my suffering by. But you are not one of them!' " (Last Scene, Chapter IV). Collins had neither escaped nor resolved the ambiguities of his situation as a writer; he had only exploited them.

III *Armadale*

Armadale (1866) represents a departure from the line of development suggested by its predecessor. Except for occasional comments upon the inconsistencies of the law and for an exposure of the dangers implicit in the private control of sanitariums, *Armadale* reveals only slight preoccupation with social disorder. Resisting classification more than any of Collins' other novels, it is primarily an exploration of the nature of guilt, both personal and inherited. If the conclusions implied in the novel are less than clear, the fact may simply reflect Collins' own uncertainty about aspects of man's relation to the evil around him.

Although in our own century T. S. Eliot was to express firm admiration for *Armadale*,[6] at the time of its publication the book was deplored by some critics, largely because Lydia Gwilt, in radiant beauty at thirty-five, passes unmarred through her various sins. Toward the end of the narrative Lydia commits suicide, but to the time of that action she is sustained, if not as "the heroine" that the reviewer in *The Spectator* called her,[7] at least as the most sympathetic of villainesses. And Allan Armadale himself, but partially and ironically the titular character, finds security from the powers of evil only because of the intervention of another. Although Collins in some measure created a myth about evil that implicitly echoes the story of Original Sin, he did not in any way build his story upon the middle-class belief in self-dependence and in the reward that follows the personal exercise of virtue. The fact that many of the characters bear the burden of guilt bestowed upon them by their fathers precludes as a significant possibility the appeal to the values of the middle class.

Described by Collins' biographer Kenneth Robinson as "labyrinthine," [8] the plot of *Armadale* rests upon the fact that two young men, like their fathers before them, can lay claim to the name "Allan Armadale"; only one uses the name—the other employs various means to prevent the world from knowing who he is. Thus, the title of *Armadale* is to some extent ironic, like that of *The Woman in White* in posing the problem of identifying its own referent; in this case, the action of the plot asks this question: What does it mean to be Allan Armadale?

The question is compounded by the fact that, many years before the principal action, the father of one of the young men murdered in vengeance the father of the other. Ultimately ignoring his father's deathbed wish that he avoid all contact with the other young Armadale, the son of the murderer, passing as "Ozias Midwinter," devotes his mature efforts to masking his real identity and at the same time protecting the sense of identity of Allan Armadale, the ineffectual and passive son of the man his father had murdered. The foil of Ozias Midwinter, even when ultimately his wife, is Lydia Gwilt herself; the missing maid of Allan Armadale's mother, Lydia has now returned after many years of crime. Essentially in response to her contrivance against Allan Armadale, the plot proceeds, with Midwinter serving in his protective role.

Trusting and cheerful, a simple and childlike man, Allan Armadale exists on the primary level of perception; he is aware of things but has no sense of the complexity of the situations surrounding him; he reduces the human personality to the attributes composing it. Response to the apparent friendliness of people sets the limits of his conscious involvement in the events that comprise his story: his befriending Ozias Midwinter; his mother's death and his inheritance of Thorpe Ambrose; his engagement to Miss Milroy and his capitulation to Miss Gwilt; Midwinter's later marriage to her; one attempt on his life when his own yacht is scuttled by a villainous crew; and the final attempt to murder him, made by Lydia Gwilt after his reconciliation with Miss Milroy.

Lydia exists at a much higher level of comprehension: she is aware of persons as composite realities, of the events in which they participate, and of the potential they offer for her exploitation. If there is a quality of the unfallen Adam in Allan Armadale, there is in Lydia Gwilt something of the intense predatory terror known to Eve the moment after her fall, when she fully realized that she must contrive to make Adam follow. Initially, it is indeed Allan Armadale whom Lydia plots to marry. When her plan is thwarted, she marries Midwinter under his own but concealed real name, Allan Armadale, so that, planning to murder the recognized Allan and then to deny Midwinter, she can point to the record of her marriage to "Allan Armadale" and claim a vast inheritance as the widow. Twice foiled in her attempts upon the life of Allan, Lydia Gwilt saves Midwinter from death because her sins have made her not so much repentant as weary; then she dies.

Only Ozias Midwinter, son of the man who could truly claim the Armadale name and murdered him who adopted it, has a level of awareness sufficient to comprehend and defeat the schemes of Lydia Gwilt. Initially grateful that Allan Armadale has saved him from the effects of exposure and starvation, Midwinter innocently learns of the sin of his father; his gratitude to Allan is transformed into an intense drive toward expiation. His position is enunciated much later, in the last letter that he receives from the Reverend Decimus Brock, who has been the friend to Allan Armadale and who has sustained the relationship between Allan and Midwinter. "Remember, if that time [of trouble] comes, that I died firmly disbelieving in your influence over Allan being other than an influence for good," Brock writes in his final illness, "The great sacrifice of the Atonement—I say it reverently—has its moral reflections, even in this world. If danger ever threatens Allan, you, whose father took his father's life—YOU, and no other, may be the man whom the providence of God has appointed to save him" (Book III, Chapter XIV).

The moral burden now belongs entirely to Midwinter—his father's confession has been long-destroyed, and, with the death of Mr. Brock, no testimony remains that the murder was ever committed. A more real Armadale than the man to whom he hereafter acts as a savior, Midwinter, who comprehends the meaning rather than merely the constituents of experience, more than matches Lydia Gwilt in her designs upon the innocent Allan. Midwinter's marriage to Lydia, taking place not long after the death of Mr. Brock, assumes something of the quality of the ritual of sacrifice— his atonement for the sins of his father. He thereby takes upon himself, under his rightful name of "Armadale," the suffering and perhaps the destruction intended for his friend. And she who has planned the death of Armadale now derives from the anticipation of her marriage to his surrogate not so much malign satisfaction as a momentary awareness of the pervasive effect of Midwinter's goodness. "I have won the great victory; I have trampled my own wickedness under foot," Lydia writes on the eve of her wedding. "I am innocent; I am happy again" (Book III, Chapter XIV).

Midwinter's commitment to expiation is complicated by his fatalism, which is essentially a repudiation of Mr. Brock's providentialism; he firmly believes that he is doomed to destroy Allan Armadale just as his own father destroyed Allan's. Caught between the two forces, Midwinter becomes indeed a suffering Messiah, feeling the incapacity to achieve what he knows he must strive for. Allan Armadale, aware of no more than disjointed attributes in the world of his experience and unknowingly enabled to preserve the moral image of his mother, never attains the capacity to suffer. Lydia, in the rare moments of her guilt and at the hour of her death, moved by world-weariness and her ambiguous love for Ozias Midwinter, experiences a suffering that surpasses the physical dimensions that her life has usually possessed; but only Midwinter can know its intensity.

Midwinter's fatalism is perhaps initially stimulated by reading his father's words toward the end of his confession: "Again, in the second generation, there are two Allan Armadales, as there were in the first. After working its deadly mischief with the fathers, the fatal resemblance of names has descended to work its deadly mischief with the sons" (Prologue, Chapter III). Fed by such coincidences as his being stranded with Allan Armadale on the same ship (significantly called *La Grace de Dieu*) on which his own father had murdered Allan's, Midwinter's belief in the operations of a malign fate assumes its fullest expression in the prophetic interpretation that he imposes upon a complex dream of Allan Armadale.

Counterpoised to Midwinter's view is that of Mr. Hawbury, a medical man specializing in the activities of the mind, which—in its assumption of recognizably causative factors in the waking experiences of the dreamer—is strikingly consistent with the views to be developed in the late nineteenth and early twentieth centuries. "There is nothing at all extraordinary in my theory of dreams: it is the theory accepted by the great mass of my profession," Mr. Hawbury remarks.

"A dream is the reproduction, in the sleeping state of the brain, of images and impressions produced on it in the waking state; and this reproduction is more or less involved, imperfect, or contradictory, as the action of certain faculties in the dreamer is controlled more or less completely by the influence of sleep. Without inquiring further into this latter part of the subject—a very curious and interesting part of it—let us take the theory, roughly and generally, as I have just stated it, and apply it at once to the dream now under consideration." He took up the written paper from the table, and dropped the formal tone (as of a lecturer addressing an audience) into which he had insensibly fallen. "I see one event already in this dream," he resumed, "which I know to be the reproduction of a waking impression produced on Mr. Armadale in my own presence. If he will only help me by exerting his memory, I don't despair of tracing back the whole succession of events set down here to something that he has said or thought, or seen or done, in the four-and-twenty hours, or less, which preceded his falling asleep on the deck of the timber ship." (Book I, Chapter V)

The sensibility reflected here, with its repudiation of supernaturalism, is akin to Collins', though it was one hardly shared by a majority of his readers. Ozias Midwinter, in his commitment to atonement for the sins of his father, reflects and increases the virtue he has attained, but the terms in which he casts his commitment—the symbols through which he gives it order and expression—need not have intrinsic truth or validity in order for the good that he does to be real.

The plot of *Armadale* works out in rational terms the events which the most significantly moral character attributes to higher causes. The author imposed neither the rational nor the fatalistic explanation upon his readers. Using the narrative method so highly developed in *The Woman in White*, Collins allowed individual characters in *Armadale* to emerge through their own statements, which they frequently do against a background that could impose only a somewhat ironic construction upon their very words. A multiplicity of orientations was the result, each partaking to some degree of one of the two opposing views of reality. The reader who made a commitment to one of them might well be judged by the nature of that commitment. But Collins, intellectually disposed toward Mr. Hawbury and in moral agreement with Ozias Midwinter, could remain detached.

CHAPTER 5

The Major Novels, 1868–70

I *The Moonstone*

OF the two novels for which Wilkie Collins has been best known, *The Moonstone* (1868) has perhaps received more attention than *The Woman in White* because it is regarded as the first English detective novel. In fact, Dorothy L. Sayers described it as "probably the very finest detective story ever written." [1] At times, however, the various aspects of the quality of the book are obscured by considerations of its historical position in the development of a particular *sous-genre*. Admittedly a triumph in the exploitation of man's rational faculty for fictional purposes, as indeed all significant detective stories must be, it also utilizes, as a means of explaining the mystery that reason seeks to solve, the potential offered by the nether side of the human mind: it becomes one of the first major works in the fiction of the unconscious.

Between the two extreme aspects of man's response stands man himself—and that he is neither wholly rational nor fully reacting below the level of consciousness is presented here with extraordinary skill. Rarely in the nineteenth century have the ambiguities of individual character, set against a partly incomprehensible world, been more clearly revealed than in the protracted dramatic monologues of such characters in *The Moonstone* as Gabriel Betteredge and Druscilla Clack. Most obscured has been the seriousness of *The Moonstone*, which implies the question that from the collapse of the Enlightenment, the committed literary artist has increasingly asked: What is the nature of identity or of the Self, and for what must it be held responsible?

The novel was immediately successful, both in England and America—where, despite Harper and Brothers' best calculations, four pirated editions appeared to compete with that of the publisher. [2] Of particular importance among the factors contributing to the success of the novel may be the general absence of social

criticism, overt or implied. Although the Evangelicalism of Miss
Druscilla Clack dominates her narrative, it is so extreme in the
expressions that it assumes that few of even the most extreme
readers would be likely to see themselves in the portrait. Similarly, few more who had attained sufficient freedom to read novels
at all would explicitly disagree with Ezra Jennings' antisabbatar-
ian remark about "the established Sunday tyranny, . . . one of
the institutions of this free country, [which] so times the trains as
to make it impossible to ask any body to travel to us [on that day]
from London" (Extracted from the Journal of Ezra Jennings).

The philosophic implications lying at the base of the question of
identity posed by the narrative, ultimately devastating to the belief of a large number of readers, exist too far below the surface of
the narrative itself to be grasped. For Collins' public, therefore,
The Moonstone was without ambiguities; a work posing no unpleasant questions, it might be trusted to entertain. Tightly constructed as it is, *The Moonstone* sustained the readers at an almost
consistently high level of response to the game of reason and motive which they saw the characters playing. In its presentation of
the game itself, it was a serious work which set the standard for
the detective novels that were to follow.

The emergence of the detective story as a literary form is a
characteristic development of the nineteenth century. In the English tradition there had been the Newgate Calendar—the profit-
able recording and publication by "the Ordinary Chaplain" of the
stories told by those poor souls, like Moll Flanders' comrades, who
were about to go "out of the world by the steps and the string";
and from this developed a fiction of rogues and villains, of which
Fielding's *Jonathan Wild the Great* (1743) was an early instance.
There had also been the Gothic novel and the tales of terror, emphasizing the mystery and sometimes the supernatural elements
not part of the literature of criminal life. Adapting the tale of
terror to the novel of ideas in *Caleb Williams* (1794), William
Godwin brought to the English tradition a novel depending for its
resolution upon the characters' rational activity.

To this point the English tradition failed to repudiate popular
hostility to the police and the representatives of authority, pre-
served even by the middle classes from the long centuries of op-
pression by aristocratic government. For the detective novel to
develop significantly, the image of the police had first to become

unsullied in the popular mind. The English popularity of the *Mémoires* of François-Jules Vidocq (1775–1857), published in Paris in 1829, did much to establish the figure of the detective as an agent of good; and the emerging middle-class readers increasingly depended for their survival as a group upon the enforcement of law. Nevertheless, the official policeman remained sufficiently tainted that a compromise was often reached in detective fiction that was expressed by the use of a private detective or, as in *The Moonstone*, a police officer from outside the immediate region. The development of a new kind of fiction thus established also depended upon the growth of a large reading public that made possible the expansion of the novel itself, but in this instance the readers had to have developed their rational capacities sufficiently to be able to follow the logical sequence on which the solution rested.

Finally, the detective story offered a means by which those as yet unprepared or unwilling to face the ethical implications of some of the leading ideas of the nineteenth century could retain the traditional differentiation between good and evil without concerning themselves with the question of the validity of the ontological structure on which such a differentiation implicitly rests. No work illustrates this fact so much as *The Moonstone*, which, when it is read exclusively at the level of action, remains a detective story and does not really press the implications of the meaning of identity or of the nature of moral responsibility. Stated another way, the detective story implies the grounds of its own existence: that, by the exercise of reason to discover and destroy some form of evil, man might attain good—an implication which is thereafter subject to no very close scrutiny. The question of the reason for the existence of evil in the first place remains unvoiced, as does the proposal that somehow, after triumphing over evil, the individual may achieve a state higher than that which he had experienced before he encountered evil. And, for those few readers ordinarily moved by intellectual doubt, the firm and rationalized distinction between good and evil might continue as part of the work of fiction and offer to its readers a form of satisfaction not found in the same way in life or in other intellectual activities.

The method which Collins brought near perfection in *The Woman in White*, by which the narrative is developed through the protagonist's editing of individual documents, was clearly suited to the needs of the kind of fiction given direction by *The Moonstone*. Encountering a group of dramatic monologues significantly arranged, the reader is able to learn more about the total situation than any one of the active characters knows.[3] In *The Moonstone*, Franklin Blake, who is in love with his cousin Rachel Verinder, collects statements by those who have witnessed or participated in the episode of the disappearance of the Moonstone—the gem once stolen by Rachel's uncle, John Herncastle, from an idol in a Brahmin temple—on the night of Rachel's birthday, when, according to the terms of her uncle's will, it had been presented to her. Although each narrator brings to his story his own moral orientation, nothing is imposed upon the total narrative beyond the demonstration of the ultimate innocence of Franklin Blake himself—long suspected as the *premeditating* thief—and the identification of the real criminal. Despite the fact that the narrator of the Prologue, who details the original theft of the stone, foresees that the "crime brings its own fatality with it," the succeeding events result entirely from human agency. In the end, only Franklin Blake is in the position to impose meaning upon the full episode, but, perhaps with deference to the presumably equal judgment of his readers, he refrains.

The principal quality of the resulting narrative structure is the organic unity that is derived to a great degree from the exploitation of either the dramatic irony or the incomplete knowledge apparent in nearly every individual narration. Rachel Verinder writes to Ezra Jennings not long before the crucial experiment is conducted upon Franklin Blake: "I want to have something to do with it, even in the unimportant character of a mere looker-on" (Extracted from the Journal of Ezra Jennings). She here describes the situation to some degree of each of the participants in the episode: in terms of deducible meaning, none is really more than "a mere looker-on." Even the villain, Godfrey Ablewhite, begins his involvement by watching what is in front of him, and makes the significant commitment only somewhat later. Sergeant Cuff, in his letter of explanation to Franklin Blake—reconstructing the moment when the unknowingly drugged Blake took the Moonstone so that he might protect Rachel from the three Indians pledged to its recovery—remarks of the ultimate thief of the gem: "In that position he [Godfrey Ablewhite] not only detected you in taking the Diamond out of the drawer—he also detected Miss

Verinder silently watching you from her bedroom, through her open door. He saw that *she* saw you take the Diamond too" (Sergeant Cuff's Narrative, Chapter IV). The very *seeing*, a form of *knowing*, gives each character a degree of power in relation to other characters, each of whom may in return have a species of knowledge about him. The structure of the total narrative resembles an arrangement of mirrors reflecting mirrors, no one of which directly reflects full reality.

In some instances, dramatic irony arises from the fact that the narrator's total viewpoint is insufficiently complex to comprehend the significance of what he experiences or reveals. Thus, Gabriel Betteredge, judging Sergeant Cuff entirely by appearances that do not conform to Betteredge's image of what Cuff should be, distrusts him:

A fly from the railway drove up as I reached the lodge; and out got a grizzled, elderly man, so miserably lean that he looked as if he had not got an ounce of flesh on his bones in any part of him. He was dressed all in decent black, with a white cravat round his neck. His face was as sharp as a hatchet, and the skin of it was as yellow and dry and withered as an autumn leaf. His eyes, of a steely light gray, had a very disconcerting trick, when they encountered your eyes, of looking as if they expected something more from you than you were aware of yourself. His walk was soft; his voice was melancholy; his long lanky fingers were hooked like claws. He might have been a parson, or an undertaker, or any thing else you like, except what he really was. A more complete opposite to Superintendent Seegrave than Sergeant Cuff, and a less comforting officer to look at for a family in distress, I defy you to discover, search where you may (Gabriel Betteredge's Narrative, Chapter XII).

And the evangelical old maid, Druscilla Clack, secure in the deep sense of her own rectitude, learns nothing from any experience. Elsewhere, the narrator, though acquiring information in the course of the events recalled, has as yet insufficient knowledge to interpret it correctly. The narrative of Mr. Matthew Bruff, the solicitor, serves as a device to bring together certain strands of information that are to be fully exploited by others.

The traditional literary juxtaposition of reality and appearance is a significant aspect of the method informing *The Moonstone;* yet the appearance of Sergeant Cuff, whose very strength as a character comes from his lack of flamboyance, has misled some of the modern critics as well as Gabriel Betteredge.[4] Each character, operating within the structure of the novel, must continually discriminate between what is real and what merely appears to be; not every confusion of the two is so humorous as Betteredge's judgment of Cuff. Rosanna Spearman, possessing the half-knowledge that is more deceptive than total ignorance, tragically misunderstands Franklin Blake's *apparent* snub of her. Ezra Jennings, Mr. Candy's inventive assistant, is the most striking instance of the confusion of appearance and reality in the human person. Franklin Blake, recurringly upset at seeing Jennings ("the man with the piebald hair twice in one day!" [Franklin Blake's Narrative, Chapter VI]), develops a compulsion to find some means to identify this man who will actually identify Blake—that is, return to Blake his moral identity by revealing the capacities of his unconscious self to be amoral.

To the ordinary reader of 1868, the juxtaposition between appearance and reality would have no further importance than in the deception marking the activities of certain characters, with the resulting momentary confusion of the reader in his attempts to distinguish between the "good" and the "bad" characters. Beyond this point such a reader would not go; he was unconcerned. But in this novel, in the dramatic and ironic manipulation of character, in the exploration of the reality of the self lying beneath the personality, Collins reflected some of the serious intellectual concerns of his age.[5]

Gabriel Betteredge, the aging house-steward to Lady Verinder, the man whose narratives follow the Prologue and precede the Epilogue, is one of the most striking of the characters through whom the relation of several sensibilities is explored. Apparently a patient and long-suffering husband of a shrewish wife—in whose departure from life he finds reason to infer the reality of "an all-wise Providence"—and a devoted father, Betteredge has passed through life entirely unable, except in matters related to survival, to distinguish between appearance and reality; and his world view is the accumulation of the intellectual fragments cast forth by several passing centuries. He is fully aware of his role as narrator, but, with an even intensified irony, he cannot recognize how truthfully he writes when he remarks, "I am asked to tell the story of the Diamond, and, instead of that, I have been telling the story

of my own self. Curious, and quite beyond me to account for"
(Gabriel Betteredge's Narrative, Chapter II).

Betteredge's classic misvaluation of Sergeant Cuff is reflected in
his handling of other characters, notably Godfrey Ablewhite,
whom he introduces, and Rosanna Spearman, whom he rightfully
regards as innocent but for the wrong reasons. He can approach
what he believes is an understanding of the sophisticated Franklin
Blake only by reducing him to a composite of national roles and
by attributing a given action to the momentary supremacy of "the
German side" or "the French side." With his important place in
the hierarchy below stairs, Gabriel Betteredge is a man whose
learning has been esteemed by those whom he directs; he is accustomed to making pronouncements and completely believes in the
authority of what he says. If he has not read widely, he has read
repeatedly in the works that support and strengthen his own point
of view; his narrative is, somewhat pompously, calculated to reflect the wisdom born of this reading.[6]

Yet, his narrative reflects, more than all else, the fact that Betteredge remains totally simplistic in his view of life. An empiricist
in his consideration of all that he regards as practical affairs, Betteredge considers himself "a good Protestant" who is ever mindful
of his moral duty (Gabriel Betteredge's Narrative, Chapter XV).
His world view rests upon a firm belief in Christian revelation
tempered by a flexible commitment to the proposition that by the
exercise of reason man can triumph over all adversity. Not surprisingly, Betteredge has taken as his guide in life Defoe's *Robinson
Crusoe* (1719), itself a monumental fusion of Protestant providentialism and empirical rationalism.[7]

Though he has worn out a number of copies, Betteredge does
not regard the *whole* book as a significant comment upon human
experience so much as he uses it as Crusoe himself used the Bible,
opening it at random to a passage which he then takes as a comment upon his situation of the moment because, as he asserts, he
has been led to this passage by providential means. Avowedly
anticlerical and insistently "not superstitious" (Chapter I), Gabriel Betteredge has established *Robinson Crusoe* as an indisputable authority that only he can interpret, a substitute for Scriptures bestowed by the Enlightenment upon those modern beings
who, failing to discriminate between their reason and their faith,
lost all real sense of the value of either.

Betteredge becomes an amiable parody of the woman whose fundamentalism he so despises, Druscilla Clack. As she judges others by their reactions to her use of Scriptures, Gabriel judges men by their response to *Robinson Crusoe*: Ezra Jennings is to be pitied because he has not read the book since childhood, and Franklin Blake is to be esteemed after he appears to have accepted the providential usefulness of Defoe's novel. And in the conclusion of his first, and major, portion of narrative, Gabriel Betteredge demonstrates by the manner of his insistence upon the moral balance (which, in the narratives that follow, is to be seen as working through human agency) how truly incompetent he is to judge the very events that he has been recording: "May you find in these leaves of my writing what Robinson Crusoe found in his Experience on the desert island—namely, 'something to comfort yourselves from, and to set, in the description of Good and Evil, on the Credit Side of the Account.'—Farewell" (Gabriel Betteredge's Narrative, Chapter XXII). Never aware of his inability to give significant order to his experiences and ideas, Gabriel sustains his image of his own being, of the self on which all interpretation of experience must rest.

Franklin Blake, on the other hand, experiences the fragmentation of sensibility and, through the restorative activities of Ezra Jennings, is even made fully aware of the nature of his experience. Jennings' view, that the mind has faculties operating at various levels of capacity and awareness, would hardly pose for Blake a disturbing possibility.[8] In the case of the stricken Mr. Candy, now Jennings' patient, Jennings remarks upon "the superior faculty of thinking going on, more or less connectedly . . . while the inferior faculty of expression was in a state of almost complete incapacity and confusion"; with this understanding, Jennings can reconstruct the old man's meaning from fragments of speech, thereby establishing the central fact that Mr. Candy administered laudanum to the sleepless and unsuspecting Blake on the night that the Moonstone disappeared.

From this position Jennings can propose that Blake was "unconscious of what you were about when you entered the room [of Rachel Verinder]"—an idea with which Blake cannot disagree, in part because, since the moment he discovered the stain of paint upon his own nightgown, he has existed in moral alienation, unable either to endure or to explain the guilt that seems to be his.

From the time that he suspects that Ezra Jennings may be able to lead him out of his dilemma, Franklin Blake feels "physically incapable of remaining still in any one place, and morally incapable of speaking to any one human being" until Jennings can reveal his plans (Chapters IX and X). In effect, Blake has no choice but to submit to Jennings' proposed experiment, by which, through the calculated fragmentation of his personality, he might retrieve his moral identity.

The Moonstone may well be Collins' most skillfully constructed work, as it has been called, and it fully deserves its place as the first English detective novel. Of at least equal importance, however, in its use of the unconscious as the means by which reason is enabled to explain the disappearance of the Indian gem, *The Moonstone* anticipated the greater fragmentation of the sensibility of modern man, as perhaps no other major Victorian novel was to do. Paradoxically, the moment Franklin Blake rose guiltless from the fragments of his former self, the philosophic assumption on which the rational frame of the detective story rests showed evidence of collapse.

II Man and Wife

Man and Wife (1870) points toward Collins' novels of the last years, both in its preoccupation with certain social abuses and in the evidence it offers of his diminishing control over the elements in his work. Though a cause for structural weakness may lie in the fact that Collins initially conceived of the work as a play,[9] a far more demonstrable reason is the disparity between the nature of the social themes and the intensity with which Collins developed them, subordinating all other elements in the novel to their full expression. Hovering at the edge of mediocrity, *Man and Wife* is redeemed, if at all, only by several successful characterizations and by the interplay of incident and mood in revealing the moral decline of Geoffrey Delamayn.

The title has the ironic quality of several of its predecessors. Using various illustrations, real and specious, of "man and wife," the novel seeks a significant referent for the phrase, a determination of the real meaning of marriage. Three of the four principal areas of social protest relate to this intent: the Irish marriage laws, the English laws disposing of a woman's property in favor of her husband, and the Scottish marriage laws. In Collins' exploration of the dehumanizing possibilities that each of these held, he depended upon the authority, as he indicated in a footnote (Chapter XX), of the *Report of the Royal Commissioners on the Laws of Marriage*, completed for Queen Victoria and published in 1868.

Had Collins not committed himself with even greater intensity to a simultaneous protest against athleticism as a public preoccupation, he might have integrated his criticism of the marriage laws with the narrative itself. Though the moral disintegration of Geoffrey Delamayn induced by his exclusive commitment to athletic activities transforms a static situation involving many kinds of marriage into a plot, structural cohesiveness is lacking; the effect of Geoffrey's decay, though consistent in its course and expression, arises from a cause that is largely contrived.

Because intrinsic relation between athletics and moral decline is never really demonstrated, the narrator must on occasion resort to explicit assertion. "Will his skill in rowing . . . , his swiftness in running, his admirable capacity and endurance in other physical exercises, help him to win a purely moral victory over his own selfishness and his own cruelty?" he asks, with obvious rhetorical emphasis. "No! The moral and mental neglect of himself, which the material tone of public feeling about him has tacitly encouraged, has left him at the mercy of the worst instincts in his nature" (Chapter LIII). The yoking of the two themes by the character of Geoffrey Delamayn must therefore fail.

The narrative falls into two parts. Like that of *Armadale*, it concerns a relationship, in this instance between two young women, imposed upon the present generation by its parents. In the summer of 1831, two childhood friends are separating, Blanche to go to India and become a governess and Anne to be trained for the stage. Twenty-four years later, Anne, now married to John Vanborough, has a twelve-year-old daughter, also named Anne, and is taking care of five-year-old Blanche, the daughter of Sir Thomas Lundie of India and her own old friend, for the child has been ordered to England because of her health.

John Vanborough and his wife, Anne, are living in a strained relationship, which he soon terminates, with the help of a young solicitor named Delamayn; Vanborough claims that—since he was converted to Anne's religion, Roman Catholicism, only six weeks before his wedding—his marriage of thirteen years is not valid under Irish law: "every marriage celebrated by a Popish

priest . . . between a Papist and any person who has been a
Protestant within twelve months before the marriage is declared
null and void." Vanborough remarries to further his political career, but some years later becomes a suicide; Delamayn also ad-
vances in politics and is raised to the peerage. The deserted wife
dies at the end of a year, leaving her daughter, Anne, in the care
of her friend, Lady Blanche Lundie. As her own death approaches, Lady Lundie, who has trained young Anne as her
daughter's governess, consigns Blanche to Anne's care.

In the major narrative, Sir Thomas Lundie, who had remarried
after Blanche's death, has just died, and his title has passed to his
brother Patrick, a canny Scottish attorney. The widowed Lady
Lundie has rented a Scottish country house called "Windygates,"
where Blanche is now giving a house party. Anne, ordinarily a
stable young woman, has become infatuated with, and pregnant
by, the honorable Geoffrey Delamayn, son of Mr. Vanborough's
solicitor of years past. His companion is Arnold Brinkworth, a
young heir newly engaged to Blanche. Estranged from his father,
Delamayn fears the repercussions of a public marriage; he agrees,
after Anne's threat of suicide, to wed her secretly at a quiet
nearby inn where they can marry by mutual declaration, according to the provision of Scottish law.

Before Geoffrey can follow Anne to the inn, he learns of his
father's serious illness; planning to return to London, he confides
in Arnold and sends him to the inn with a note for Anne. To avoid
embarrassing Anne, Arnold declares to the proprietess that he is
her husband, thereby possibly marrying her by his own declaration. When Geoffrey's father temporarily recovers, the son con-
sents to the family plan to have him marry a wealthy widow, Mrs.
Glenarm. At the same time he agrees to be a contestant in the
Great Footrace at Fulham. In Scotland again, to train for the race,
he learns of the Scottish provisions by which he might free himself
to marry Mrs. Glenarm by demonstrating that Arnold has married
Anne by simple declaration.

Evidence of Geoffrey's gradual moral deterioration is now apparent, but beneath the splendid athletic surface a physical deterioration induced by the moral and physical strain imposed
upon his system has also been taking place. Geoffrey collapses
during the race. Meanwhile, Arnold has married Blanche; though
he becomes aware of Geoffrey's scheme, Geoffrey's own declara-

tion to Anne constituting marriage is exposed, and the scheme now falters. The laws which have freed Arnold from all obligation to Anne (whose baby has meanwhile been lost) have simultaneously placed her in the control of Geoffrey, who now appears to accept her as his wife. Actually, he secretly plans, with the help of the terrorized Hester Dethridge (his cook, over whom he has power because he has the secret of her own murder of a brutal husband), to murder Anne and free himself to marry Mrs. Glenarm. Though Geoffrey approaches success, Hester, resolving her conflict between morality and physical survival, turns upon him and destroys him. She is sent to an asylum; Arnold and Blanche await an heir; and Sir Patrick Lundie, who has consistently imposed order on the world for which he has assumed responsibility, marries Anne.

Had Collins been willing to assume rather than explain Geoffrey's condition, allowing him to be motivated by the simple love for money, a common denominator among modern social appetites, he could have brought to the array of marriages the interaction that the plot demands. The cause as it stands is, both clinically and fictionally, hardly demonstrable. The resulting plot, without significant conflict beyond the subdued battle of wits between Sir Patrick and Geoffrey, depends in great measure upon an alternation between the narrator's satiric comment and his recording of brief, often ironic situations.

Early in the novel Sir Patrick describes Geoffrey's principal attributes as his class, his education, and his athletic prowess: "having won the highest popular distinction which the educational system of modern England can bestow—he had pulled the stroke-oar in a University boat-race. Add to this, that nobody had ever seen him read any thing but a newspaper." Somewhat later, Geoffrey's deplorable intellectual condition is amusingly, if predictably, illustrated as Sir Patrick addresses his sister-in-law:

"Lady Lundie," he answered, "you read me like a book." To the astonishment of all persons present under forty he emphasized those words by laying his hand on his heart, and quoting poetry. "I may say with Dryden," added the gallant old gentleman:

> "'Old as I am, for ladies' love unfit,
>   The power of beauty I remember yet.'"

Lady Lundie looked unaffectedly shocked. Mr. Delamayn went a step further. He interfered on the spot—with the air of a man who feels himself imperatively called upon to perform a public duty.

"Dryden never said that," he remarked, "I'll answer for it."

Sir Patrick wheeled round with the help of his ivory cane, and looked Mr. Delamayn hard in the face.

"Do you know Dryden, sir, better than I do?" he asked.

The Honorable Geoffrey answered, modestly, "I should say I did. I have rowed three races with him, and we trained together."

Sir Patrick looked round him with a sour smile of triumph.

"Then let me tell you, sir," he said, "that you trained with a man who died nearly two hundred years ago."

Mr. Delamayn appealed, in genuine bewilderment, to the company generally:

"What does this old gentleman mean?" he asked. "I am speaking of Tom Dryden, of Corpus. Every body in the University knows *him.*"

"I am speaking," echoed Sir Patrick, "of John Dryden the Poet. Apparently, every body in the University does *not* know *him!*" (Chapter II)

Expectedly, Sir Patrick becomes the spokesman for the authorial point of view, urging the national implications of the sports to which Geoffrey is disastrously committed. "He presumes to exist," Sir Patrick remarks after Arnold has inquired about the nature of Geoffrey's offense:

"Don't stare! I am speaking generally. Your friend is the model young Briton of the present time. I don't like the model young Briton. I don't see the sense of crowing over him as a superb national production, because he is big and strong, and drinks beer with impunity, and takes a cold shower-bath all the year round. There is far too much glorification in England, just now, of the mere physical qualities which an Englishman shares with the savage and the brute. And the ill results are beginning to show themselves already! We are readier than we ever were to practice all that is rough in our national customs, and to excuse all that is violent and brutish in our national acts. Read the popular books—attend the popular amusements; and you will find at the bottom of them all a lessening regard for the gentler graces of civilized life, and a growing admiration for the virtues of the aboriginal Britons!" (Chapter III)

Delightful though he may appear as a fictional personality, Sir Patrick rather stiffly assumes the role of prophet imposed upon him. Intellectually he is melioristic, believing that mankind has progressed through civilizing centuries from a barbarous state which still lies at the base of every man's being and, if the individual is not conditioned by the influences of civilization, will reveal itself by his predatory impingement upon his fellows. Sir Patrick's conclusions, consistent with Collins' view of the relative nature of virtue and vice, are not that Geoffrey Delamayn is *immoral* so much as *amoral*, unconditioned for the moral experience. "There has been nothing in his training to soften the barbarous hardness in his heart, and to enlighten the barbarous darkness in his mind," Sir Patrick remarks of Geoffrey. "Temptation finds this man defenseless, when temptation passes his way . . . he is, to all moral intents and purposes, an Animal, and nothing more" (Chapter XIX).

When amoral action is cast within a social context, however, it necessarily appears to be immoral. And in a literary record of an individual supremely unaware of the moral possibility, caught in a gradually intensifying situation that demands of him the choice that he is unprepared to make, his course would appear to be one of moral deterioration. Geoffrey Delamayn, nevertheless, determines upon certain actions—from the slightly irregular plan for a momentarily secret marriage to Anne to the complex contrivance for her murder—only in response to the increasingly complex situations in which he finds himself; he is not a spontaneous villain, delighting in his own evil or in the suffering of others. Rather, like one of George Eliot's victims of the inexorable results of his own inadequate decisions (such as Tito Melema in *Romola* [1862–63]), Geoffrey Delamayn ostensibly falls away from the moral standards of his society; adjusting means to ends and wishing merely to survive socially and economically, he is unable to resist (in fact, he is unaware of the viable possibility of resistance itself) the course most accessible to him. Distinguished from the causes of his moral failure in the particular kind of training he has received, the record itself of the moral failure becomes one of the redeeming aspects of the novel.

Juxtaposed to Geoffrey as a character in the final action is Hester Dethridge, the former cook of Lady Lundie, who, appearing "dumb" to all around her, carries the secret of her own bad marriage that terminated in her impulsive murder of her husband. With her own pathetic story serving as an answer to Geoffrey's pompous outcry ("Shame on the people who interfere between man and wife! Shame!" [Chapter LI]), Hester emerges more significantly in moral judgment upon Geoffrey than in social judgment upon the institutions of her fellows, for which she was largely intended. A great mass of a woman conceived in mythic rather than mimetic terms, Hester in her mute alienation experiences the moral crisis that Geoffrey can never comprehend. Thus, as she looks upon him in silent judgment, he can move to but one conclusion about her: "'Mad!' he thought—and turned his back on the sight of her" (Chapter XXI). That society finally concurs and confines her for life to an asylum may constitute as full a judgment upon society as upon Hester, especially since by this time the institutions of society have been revealed as at least inconsistent. Hester Dethridge is one of the few characters in the novel capable of moral crisis and therefore of reflecting the significant deficiency in the awareness of Geoffrey Delamayn.

Living in self-imposed dumbness, so that she will not be forced to reveal the past life on which she cannot yet impose a moral resolution, Hester approaches self-containment, illustrated by the passiveness—"the sinister tranquillity" (Chapter VIII)—with which she responds to her dismissal by Lady Lundie. About her is a grotesque sacramentalism, evident in her restoration of Anne, who has fainted in the library at Windygates: "The instant Hester Dethridge touched her, the swooning woman gave signs of life" (Chapter XXII). The moment foretells Hester's ultimate act, in the resolution of the moral struggle that has possessed her long before it was compounded by Geoffrey's power over her, when, to save Anne's life and thereby to absolve herself from the guilt of her husband's death, she attacks Geoffrey at the crucial moment in his plan to murder Anne.

Whatever reorientation follows the resolution of her conflict, Hester attains it outside the pale of society's comprehension. She is judged not so much guilty of murder as afflicted with insanity, for which she is confined. Doubtless, this solution quietly satisfied a majority of Collins' audience, hardly suspecting that in her violent moment of moral resolution Hester Dethridge excluded from further contact with herself a morally inconsistent society.

CHAPTER 6

Uneven Shadows

I The Nature of Decline

THE proposal that the work of Wilkie Collins from 1870 to the time of his death in 1889 is marked by evidence of progressive deterioration is too facile a comment upon a situation which, though perhaps not overly complex in its manifestations, was inconsistent in its development. The last novel, *Blind Love*, for example, while not in any way a major work, is superior in structure and characterization to its immediate predecessors. Though none of the novels even approaches the sturdy works of the 1860's, perhaps only one or two seems completely deficient in the qualities abundantly found in the major novels.

In one of the better achievements of these years, *Poor Miss Finch* (1872), the central situation has significant overtones concerning the nature of the relation of the individual self to the outer world as that relationship is sustained by sight or the lack of it. In *The Law and the Lady* (1875), *Jezebel's Daughter* (1880), and *The Black Robe* (1881), incident develops with sufficient rapidity and integrity to sustain the narrative. *The New Magdalen* (1873), a kind of modern social allegory, poses with some degree of irony the question of the possibility that society allows for moral revival. The attainment in each of these instances, however, fails to be integrated with the rest of the novel. The complexity and control which mark *The Woman in White, No Name,* or *The Moonstone* are no longer apparent in the novels of the late years. In the very narratives themselves, incident tends to become lineal rather than parallel in its development; in place of the almost overwhelming multiplicity of facets in the plot of *Armadale* or *Man and Wife*, there is a simplicity of structure that probably does little to sustain interest beyond the moment of the reading itself.

The shorter fiction, certainly the novelettes of the last two decades, does not reveal quite such marked effects of Collins' declining powers as do the novels. Despite the excellence *in kind* attained in *Gabriel's Marriage* and in *Sister Rose,* the potential for achievement in the complex ordering of many elements of a work of fiction is more limited in the shorter form; certainly, none of Collins' novelettes ever approaches the achievement of *The Woman in White* or *The Moonstone.* Of the six novelettes which Collins published during the last years, those which approach total failure, *My Lady's Money* (1877) and *The Guilty River* (1886), do so because of the selection and the particular treatment of subject rather than because of inability to integrate the elements of the work to the extent that the subject allows.

The general causes for Collins' failure to maintain the level of attainment marking the work of the 1860's are not difficult to suggest: his increasing ill-health, his growing dependence upon laudanum as a means of controlling his pain, and finally his commitment to the fiction of social purpose. The relative impact of these causes, so confidently evaluated by a number of critics, cannot be measured. Pain and the effect of drugs are personal long before they become social factors, and what they do to undermine the literary achievement must remain incommunicable except to the literary work itself; and the esthetic deterioration attendant upon the commitment to social criticism is an assumption as much as a fact, noticeably consistent with the critical position of those who emphasized it in the case of Collins. Collins did fail to maintain his achievement, a fact which, whatever its cause might have been, is of course regrettable; not only did the man outlive his genius, but the uneven shadows of his failure in the last years have absorbed for posterity the brightness of his earlier attainments.

II *The Novels, 1870–90*

Regarded by the critics in both Collins' day and our own as generally contrived, *Poor Miss Finch* (1872) was at the time of its publication hardly a success with the public. The plot does not contain what might conceivably be popular incident, and, in the years since the publication of the novel and the death of Collins, the one question of intellectual significance posed by the novel has probably been obscured by the contrivance of the plot.

In the narrative, Madame Pratolungo, the widow of a South American socialist, accepts a position as companion to Miss Lu-

cilla Finch, an attractive young lady who has been blind since the
early years of her childhood. Mr. Oscar Dubourg appears in the
neighborhood and is soon engaged to Lucilla. Developing epilep-
tic fits, Oscar learns that the only treatment for these is by silver
nitrate injection, which, he is told, will turn his skin blue. He sub-
mits, though he plans to keep his disfigurement from Lucilla, who,
presumably, will never see him.

Nugent Dubourg, Oscar's identical twin, just returned from
America, suggests that Lucilla be examined by Herr Grosse, a
doctor who has successfully operated in other seemingly hopeless
cases of blindness. Wanting only to see Oscar, Lucilla insists on
the operation. Meanwhile, Nugent has fallen in love with Lucilla;
after the seemingly successful operation, by confusing identities
and by exploiting Lucilla's inherent dislike for things of a dark
color, he nearly marries her. Fortunately for Oscar, the operation
is but partially successful, and Lucilla falls again into blindness;
the deceptive brother is foiled by Madame Pratolungo on the eve
of his marriage, and the two lovers are reunited.

Certain elements in *Poor Miss Finch* are by this time familiar.
Nugent is no villain in any absolute sense, but, like Geoffrey
Delamayn, he moves from one amoral commitment to another
until he has reached the point that he expresses himself in acts
which society must regard as immoral. And, after his failure, Nugent goes forth as an explorer upon an essentially expiational journey that ends in his death. His brother and sister-in-law are then
able to forgive him and to name their first child after him. Oscar
Dubourg is rather typical of a certain kind of Collins protagonist;
he is passive to the circumstances around him and to the directions of his own emotions, at least to the point of crisis, revealing
like Basil and Allan Armadale "the immovable obstinacy of a
weak man" (Chapter XXII). At least some elements seem gratuitous, such as the intensely avowed socialism of Madame Pratolungo, who, as enveloping narrator, unconvincingly draws upon
her political beliefs for her motivation in various responses and
decisions.

In the somewhat uneven intimations about the nature of personal identity found in *Poor Miss Finch,* the novel approaches
intellectual significance. "Experience was yet to show me that the
blind can live in their imaginations, and have their favorite fancies
and illusions like the rest of us," Madame Pratolungo comments

early in her narrative (Chapter III). Much of the action that follows depends upon Lucilla Finch's negative response to dark objects, specifically of course to the "blue man" she sees after her sight has been briefly restored. However, Lucilla has been blind since she was one year old, so that she has never *experienced* darkness; to her it is primarily an idea rather than an image, which she associates with her own experience only when it is extrinsically introduced. "So far as I can see, she fails to discover intuitively the presence of dark people in a room, or of dark colors in the ornaments of a room," Nugent remarks to Madame Pratolungo, moving to the conception through which he will operate in his attempt to substitute himself for Oscar in Lucilla's affections. "It is only when *she is told* that such persons or such things are present that her prejudice declares itself" (Chapter XXV). The experience that follows tests the adequacy of her predisposition to express itself in judgment.

Only in the return to her blindness does Lucilla attain a meaningful recognition of reality; now she can *see* Oscar, she declares, "and I *do* see him!—as my fancy drew his picture in the first days of our love" (Chapter L). Her illusions have been judged by physical reality; but for their part, they, too, have turned in judgment upon the world that sight creates and have found it wanting. At the time that Herr Grosse holds before her newly seeing eyes the objects around them, the results of his experiments are the same: "Scarlet was not half as red—black not one-hundredth part as black—as her imagination had figured them to her in the days when she was blind. Still, as to this last color—as to black—she could feel some little encouragement. It had affected her disagreeably (just as poor Oscar's face had affected her), though she had not actually known it for the color that she disliked" (Chapter XXXIX).

That Lucilla's response is intuitively grounded is undeniable. Her brief period of sight demonstrates the dangers that such a prejudice as hers poses to human fulfillment and how void it is of rational content; after her return to blindness, she no longer retains the abstract sense of color which afflicted her before the operation; she has learned that such antipathy as hers lies no deeper than the sense which conveys the color. Freed from her abstract associations, Lucilla can now, in the renewed privation of her sense, fully attain freedom from her sense-sustained dislikes.

Thus, she comments significantly when she remarks, "My life lives in my love. And my love lives in my blindness" (Chapter L).

The story of Lucilla Finch, recalling Plato's myth of the cave as much as any other single prototype, bears great similarity to a number of other nineteenth-century works concerned with disorientation, the loss of sustaining illusions. But the import of the myth of the cave is of course that, no matter how painful, the light of the sun reveals a greater truth than is in the shadows of the cave. In the case of Lucilla Finch, one willingly returns to the darkness and elects not to try again for the light. Despite the implications, however, the conclusion of the narrative seems not to argue for the sanctity of illusions so much as for their usefulness in attaining a recognition of one's own identity—of imposing value and meaning upon the outer world irrespective of the roles that the world in turn would demand.

Before her sight is restored, Lucilla is totally dependent upon others for interpretation of occurrences around her; to this extent at least, she becomes a projection of the roles that they assume as expressive of their own social experience. With the restoration of her sight, she begins to participate with others in experiences never before shared, and on these experiences rests a new awareness of the responsibility that she now holds in society and of the role that society demands that she play. With the subsequent failure of her sight, Lucilla is able to retain the knowledge and the freedom from dependence upon others' social experiences that her period of seeing has given, but at the same time, she can escape the role that social participation has imposed upon her. Her illusions have been tempered but not lost, sustained by a vision that has been externalized. She has attained by her disorientation the recognition of her own identity.

The New Magdalen (1873), weakened by its initial conception as a play,[1] and later described by Swinburne as "merely feeble, false, and silly in its sentimental cleverness,"[2] has never been favored by critics. The subject itself, the possibility for a modern Magdalen to survive in society, may inevitably lead to the very sentimentality of which Swinburne complained; if such is the case, the fact itself gives paradoxical support to the theme of the novel: within the context of modern society, the myth springing from the Magdalen tradition is without demonstrable meaning.

The narrative of *The New Magdalen* is fairly simple, marked by neither extraneous action nor unpredictable events. Grace Rose-berry, journeying to England to become a companion to Lady Janet Roy, is pronounced dead after a shell-explosion on the Franco-Prussian frontier; near her at the time is Mercy Merrick, once a woman of the Refuge in London, who was brought from despair by the preaching of the Reverend Julian Gray and is now a Geneva Convention nurse. After a struggle of impulse and con-science, Mercy yields to the temptation to assume Grace's identity and return to England for what she now sees as the only opportu-nity that life will offer her for reacceptance into her society.

In London, believed to be Grace Roseberry, she wins a place by her own qualities not only in Lady Janet's affections but in those of Horace Holmcroft, a proper young man of the upper classes to whom she becomes engaged; only remorse keeps her from setting a date for their wedding. Unexpectedly, Julian Gray, Lady Janet's nephew, appears in the role of emissary for the real Grace Rose-berry, who has been amazingly brought back from merely the ap-pearance of death. Lady Janet and Horace immediately regard the self-righteous Grace rather than Mercy as the imposter, and it is only after Julian gradually comes to understand the situation, simultaneously falling in love with Mercy, that he brings her to confess. Horace instantly rejects Mercy as unfit, whereas Lady Janet adamantly refuses to admit the truth of her story. Mercy insists on returning to the Refuge, which she leaves to marry Ju-lian only when he has resigned his curacy, worked for a London Mission, and contracted a near-fatal fever. Julian and Mercy, the scandal of London society, sail with Lady Janet's blessings for America to start a new life.

The New Magdalen assumes most of the qualities of allegory, though the absolute standard of right on which an allegory must rest for its symbolic equations is, ironically, the moral relativism of the Reverend Julian Gray. "All sinners, my dear aunt, are more or less miserable sinners," Julian proposes to Lady Janet. "Nero must have been one of the wretchedest of mankind" (Chapter XIII). As guilt and pain are generally equitable, so the converse is true: the good that man does lives within him, bringing as its reward the will to survive and to continue to believe in mankind, despite whatever obstacles experience may cast in his way. The truth of Christianity resides, therefore, in its ethical rather than in its doc-trinal teachings; he who practices it in his own Christian society

runs the risk of the banishment that Gray himself has suffered.
And the Christian may be forced in the end, like Gray when he
resigns his curacy, to abandon the outward shows of the religious
tradition. The committed Christian in Julian Gray's position has
no choice:

"O Christ, have mercy on me!" That was her prayer—no more.
   Julian followed her. He waited a little. Then his kind hand touched
her; his friendly voice fell consolingly on her ear.
   "Rise, poor wounded heart! Beautiful, purified soul, God's angels
rejoice over you! Take your place among the noblest of God's creatures!" (Chapter XXVIII)

And Magdalen, to experience redemption in contemporary society, must become the bride of her Christ. "Who but a Pharisee can
believe that he is better than another?" Julian asks as Mercy lis-
tens. "The best among us to-day may, but for the mercy of God,
be the worst among us tomorrow. The true Christian virtue is the
virtue which never despairs of a fellow-creature. The true Christian faith believes in Man as well as in God. . . . Humanity is
sacred. Humanity has its immortal destiny" (Chapter XVII).
   Upon this position rest all significant judgments made in the
novel. The moral idea is created by man rather than bestowed
upon him (the names of the opposing female characters are,
significantly, *Grace* and *Mercy*). Lady Janet Roy, a pluralistic
representative of the Lady Bountiful tradition, powerful in her
hereditary social position, attains the *true* inner power of moral
comprehension, while society, represented by Horace Holmcroft,
excludes Magdalen and would destroy her savior. Mercy assumes
a role within the dimensions that society offers in order that she
might prove her moral identity; though she would avoid taking
what belongs to another, society gives her no other opportunity.
"What a prospect it was!" she thinks in the French dugout. "A
new identity, which she might own anywhere! a new name, which
was beyond reproach! a new past life, into which all the world
might search, and be welcome!" (Chapter IV).
   For Horace Holmcroft's allegorical role, it is important that he
hear the full account of the misfortunes that made Mercy become
what she was; then, with a resoluteness born both of the security
his place in society affords him and of his total incapacity to learn
from experience, he refuses to forgive her. He stands as the nine-

teenth-century Pharisee, repudiating by act the Christianity that he enunciates. Here and at the end of the narrative, from the viewpoint that Collins imposed upon the novel, the paradox of judgment operates: Horace Holmcroft and his society stand alone, condemned by their own harsh judgment of the "two more [added] to the number of social failures produced by England in the year of our Lord eighteen hundred and seventy-one" (Epilogue).

The Law and the Lady (1875) is the first English detective story with a female protagonist. In the narrative, Valeria Brinton marries Eustace Woodville, ignorant of the fact that under his real name, "Macallan," he has been tried in Scotland for the alleged poisoning of his first wife and has received the equivocal Scottish verdict of "Not Proven." Though Valeria understands his emotional situation, Eustace insists on leaving her; he feels that she will never again be able to trust him. Valeria, supported by her father's old clerk Benjamin, sets forth on the difficult task of proving Eustace's innocence. She first reads thoroughly the record of the trial and then plans to meet the people concerned in it. Miserrimus Dexter, a legless megalomaniac, encourages her in the supposition that Mrs. Beauly, once beloved by Eustace, is the murderer.

But Mr. Playmore, Eustace's Edinburgh attorney, suspects Dexter himself, since the invalid had developed a passion for Eustace's first wife. Considerably later, at precisely the time that Dexter slips finally into insanity, Valeria, with Benjamin present to take notes, visits Miserrimus Dexter and learns that there was once a letter that would shed light on the case; tediously recovered, the letter reveals that Eustace's first wife, long unhappy in her marriage to a man whom she had trapped into his situation, had committed suicide. Eustace, having attained an inner equilibrium by his exoneration in the eyes of Valeria, refuses to bring the letter forth as evidence of his own innocence, for, in so doing, he would sully the memory of his first wife.

The plot itself is hardly spectacular. Though the novel represents a first of its kind in the development of detective fiction, Valeria reaches her solution through happy circumstance and occasional accident more than through pure induction. The solution is hardly what the reader has been led to anticipate: suicide instead of murder. To the characters involved in the episode, re-

ward and punishment are doled forth with a regularity that seems
calculated to please even the most strict believer in poetic justice.
Eustace and Valeria presumably live in happiness to the end of
their days, secure to the point that they feel no need to reveal to
the world the document on which rests their security.

Eustace has been sufficiently punished for his love for Mrs.
Beauly during his first marriage. Sara Macallan, Eustace's first
wife, was hardly one to whom his obligation would seem strong;
in her pathetic love for him she had tricked him into the marriage
for which she paid the price of loneliness in both life and death.
Miserrimus Dexter, whose only commitment was to love rather
than to evil, for whatever evil he thereby accomplished, suffers in
pain and madness and finally death. And even Ariel, the gigantic
and grotesquely stupid woman who has been Dexter's totally
committed servant, comes to an end that is consistent with what
she did in life: not long after Dexter's funeral, she is found on his
grave, dead of cold and exposure.

The element carrying imaginative appeal to the novel and, for
what it implies, suggesting a degree of intellectual significance is
the character of Miserrimus Dexter. Hardly credible by mimetic
standards, he derives his significance from the mythic function he
serves, particularly in the context of the late nineteenth-century
preoccupation with the nature of identity. Dexter becomes a kind
of caricature of modern man in search of sustaining reality. In his
grotesque child's play he becomes the great men of the past, who,
regrettably, can meaningfully live only in the imagination of one
who is half-mad. "We kept ourselves concealed in the shadow of
the recess, and looked through the open doorway," Valeria recalls
of her first visit to Miserrimus Dexter, one of the most memorable
of Collins' scenes:

I saw (or fancied I saw, in the obscurity) a long room with a low
ceiling. The dying gleam of an ill-kept fire formed the only light by
which I could judge of objects and distances. Redly illuminating the
central portion of the room, opposite to which we were standing, the
fire-light left the extremities shadowed in almost total darkness. I
had barely time to notice this before I heard the rumbling and whistling sounds approaching me. A high chair on wheels moved by,
through the field of red light, carrying a shadowy figure with floating
hair, and arms furiously raised and lowered working the machinery
that propelled the chair at its utmost rate of speed. "I am Napoleon,

at the sunrise of Austerlitz!" shouted the man in the chair as he swept past me on his rumbling and whistling wheels, in the red glow of the fire-light. "I give the word, and thrones rock, and kings fall, and nations tremble, and men by tens of thousands fight and bleed and die!" The chair rushed out of sight, and the shouting man in it became another hero. "I am Nelson!" the ringing voice cried now. "I am leading the fleet at Trafalgar. I issue my commands, prophetically conscious of victory and death. I see my own apotheosis, my public funeral, my nation's tears, my burial in the glorious church. The ages remember me, and the poets sing my praise in immortal verse!" The strident wheels turned at the far end of the room and came back. The fantastic and frightful apparition, man and machinery blended in one —the new Centaur, half man, half chair—flew by me again in the dying light. "I am Shakespeare!" cried the frantic creature now. "I am writing *Lear,* the tragedy of tragedies. Ancients and moderns, I am the poet who towers over them all. Light! light! the lines flow out like lava from the eruption of my volcanic mind. Light! light! for the poet of all time to write the words that live forever!" He ground and tore his way back toward the middle of the room. As he approached the fire-place a last morsel of unburned coal (or wood) burst into momentary flame, and showed the open doorway. In that moment he saw us! The wheel-chair stopped with a shock that shook the crazy old floor of the room, altered its course, and flew at us with the rush of a wild animal. We drew back, just in time to escape it, against the wall of the recess. The chair passed on, and burst aside the hanging tapestry. The light of the lamp in the circular room poured in through the gap. The creature in the chair checked his furious wheels, and looked back over his shoulder with an impish curiosity horrible to see. (Chapter XXIV)

Like the creations of Dexter's imagination, all else in his world is insubstantial. The poetry he recites and the music he sings are his own, improvised, the expressions of a solipsistic world. His is the esthetic of the ultimate Romantic, rejecting the mimetic entirely for the fulfillment of the expressive. "Persons who look for mere Nature in works of Art . . . are persons to whom Mr. Dexter does not address himself," he remarks to Valeria. "He relies entirely on his imagination. Nature puts him out" (Chapter XXVII). Uninhibited in his own dark world by any other forces, social or philosophic, Dexter assumes there the role of its deity; or at least he is a Prospero transforming a Caliban into his grotesque "Ariel." The monstrous servant bearing the essential irony of identity in her name stands awkwardly at the center of Miserrimus

Dexter's world, his finest creation and the ultimate mark of all his attainment just as Hareton was Heathcliff's in Emily Brontë's *Wuthering Heights* (1847).

The two novels which followed *The Law and the Lady* were among Collins' weakest achievements. *The Two Destinies* (1876) recounts the story of the lifelong love between George Germaine, a wealthy young aristocrat, and Mary Dermody, the daughter of his father's bailiff, who, recognizing each other late in life and after many years of separation and personal trial, find happiness for the time that remains. *The Fallen Leaves—The First Series* (1879) was the least popular of any of Collins' books.[3] Described by Swinburne as "something too absurdly repulsive for comment or endurance,"[4] this novel returns to the theme of the reformed prostitute, attaining a degree of triteness and sentimentality hardly imaginable in *The New Magdalen*. The principal characters are a reforming socialist, Claude-Amelius Goldenheart and a prostitute with the even more incredible name of "Simple Sally." Understandably, no "Second Series" followed; perhaps as a mark of Collins' response to the popular failure of *The Fallen Leaves*, the next two novels to be published reveal a rapid sequence of action but very little social criticism.

Jezebel's Daughter (1880) depends heavily upon coincidence and unlikely human behavior for the development of its plot. Poison, used incidentally in *The Law and the Lady* and in *The Fallen Leaves*, is here moved to the center of action, to be adroitly manipulated by the villainess, who bears the outrageously ironic name of Madame Fontaine. In her use of poison she recalls the theme crucially developed in *The Woman in White* and *The Moonstone*, that power derives from knowledge. For only Madame Fontaine knows the secrets of both the poisons and the antidotes left by her scientist husband at his death. Whatever her shortcomings may be as a thoroughly integrated fictional character, Madame Fontaine is a representative Collins villain; she is evil to the extent that she is a hypocrite and aspires to manipulate others, in this case by having them *will* to partake of what they do not know is deadly.

Madame Fontaine, a German by origin who was once married to a Frenchman, is opposed by Mrs. Wagner, an Englishwoman of a higher sensibility; unknowingly and by this opposition, Madame Fontaine falls into the same trap she has set for others. In the

Frankfort Dead House, to which Mrs. Wagner—poisoned by Madame Fontaine and presumed dead—has been taken, Madame Fontaine, sitting with a madman and a drunken watchman, unwittingly drinks of the same poison for which the last of the antidote has been used to initiate the revival of Mrs. Wagner. The scene—in which, amid drunkenness and madness, she who has been presumed dead comes to life while she who has been living is slowly dying—characteristic of the sensation novel to which Collins was moving in his last works, expresses the ultimate purpose of, and brings the only impact to, an exciting but obviously contrived plot.

The Black Robe (1881), as much a sensation novel as its predecessor, was somewhat more successfully organized than most of Collins' later works. Developing the theme found in *The Yellow Mask* of the priest who would reclaim through inheritance the property long ago confiscated from the Church, Collins made the Jesuits as an organization the object of his attack; but partly because he countered the villainous Father Benwell by the kind and totally moral Jesuit, Arthur Penrose, he was able to avoid the pitfalls of propaganda literature. In the narrative, Lewis Romayne, pressured into fighting a duel, kills his opponent and is thereafter tortured by the voice of his victim's younger brother crying for the assassin. His friends, Lord and Lady Loring, feel that the only way to remove his burden is to lead him into a happy marriage—in this case, to their friend Stella, who was once momentarily married to a seeming villain, Winterfield, but freed by the appearance of his first wife, presumed dead.

Father Benwell, the Jesuit determined to retrieve for the Church Romayne's ancestral home, Vange Abbey (which had been confiscated by Henry VIII), moves first to convert Romayne and then to destroy his marriage to an arch-Protestant. The agent for conversion is Arthur Penrose, a Jesuit posing as a layman and serving as amanuensis to Romayne; although he accomplishes his task, the sympathetic Penrose comes to accept Romayne's marriage, which he cannot will to destroy. Benwell, however, succeeds here, persuading Romayne after his conversion that he has never really been married. Romayne leaves his wife—who, unknown to him, is now pregnant—and goes to Rome, where he becomes a priest, in time known for his passionate sermons.

Meanwhile, Winterfield has been cleared of all blame in trying to hide his first marriage from Stella and is now restored to her confidence. Romayne, whose health has been broken under the strain of work, hears of the birth of his son and, now in Paris and on his deathbed, calls Stella and the child to him. Father Benwell arrives with a codicil for Romayne to sign, assuring that Vange Abbey will return to the Church; in a moment of decision immediately before his death, Romayne gives the document to the child to throw into the fire in the room.

The plot moves quickly but suffers from an extraordinary degree of contrivance. Winterfield is perhaps the most striking example, for as a *personality* he is totally devoid of attributes; thus, as a *character* he serves entirely as a convenience. Arthur Penrose has but slightly greater structural justification. Essentially a foil to Father Benwell (who accepts quite literally the motto "The End Justifies the Means"), Penrose redeems the clergy as a group by refusing to seek any end but humanity's fulfillment.

If these characters are essentially extraneous to the development of more than the bare narrative in which they exist, so is the other strand of plot, through which Collins attempted to develop a theme of intellectual significance. This concerns the alternation between the two levels of consciousness in the young brother of the man Romayne killed in a duel. Explicitly basing his description upon an article that had appeared but two years before,[5] Collins reveals the boy in a reversal of the normal human procedure: "insane" in his physically healthy state, in which he represses a large body of experience, the boy develops a high fever, during which he recalls the substance of his repressions and "become[s] perfectly sane and reasonable." Since the story containing Father Benwell's attempts upon the Romayne property poses the question of distinguishing between legal and moral right, the theme of alternate selves in the case of the young boy might have been used to pose the additional question of the very nature of the awareness upon which the moral sense must rest. But this was not the case, and the subplot in *The Black Robe* remains essentially intrusive, abortively adding an intellectual quality to the work and probably detracting from the popular.

Heart and Science (1883) is perhaps Collins' most unfortunate work. Here, though protesting in the Preface to the first edition that he had used reliable sources, he ventured into an area of dispute, the controversy over vivisection, in which his opinions were based upon sentiment and inclination rather than upon understanding.[6] The result is extreme contrivance, by which Dr. Benjulia, who more closely than any approaches the modern scientific attitude, is made cruel and satanic, ultimately a madman. "He is said to have discontinued medical practice and devoted himself to chemical experiments," remarks one of the characters. "He has built a house in a desolate field—in some lost suburban neighborhood that nobody can discover. In plain English, Doctor Benjulia is a mystery" (Chapter XII). His antecedents are clearly Monk Lewis' Ambrosio rather than John Hunter or Edward Jenner.

Compounding the case is Mrs. Gallilee—mother of the overly sentimental and passive protagonist, Ovid Vere—whose dissection of flowers supposedly parallels Benjulia's experiments with animals. When asked if she ever reads poetry,

> Mrs. Gallilee laid herself back in her chair, and submitted patiently to her niece's simplicity. "Poetry?" she repeated, in accents of resignation. "Oh, good heavens!"
> Unlucky Carmina tried a more promising topic. "What beautiful flowers you have in the drawing-room!" she said.
> "Nothing remarkable, my dear. Everybody has flowers in their drawing-rooms—they are part of the furniture."
> "Did you arrange them yourself, aunt?"
> Mrs. Gallilee still endured it. "The florist's man," she said, "does all that. I sometimes dissect flowers, but I never trouble myself to arrange them. What would be the use of the man if I did?" This view of the question struck Carmina dumb. Mrs. Gallilee went on. "By-the-by, talking of flowers reminds one of other superfluities. Have you tried the piano in your room? Will it do?" (Chapter XV)

Within the context established in the novel, the differences between the scientist and the artist are here exploited to serve the theme of the work. Scientists are unfeeling mechanists, capable of analyzing, of cutting organism into its elements, but never of synthesizing, of creating. Scientific reasoning destroys what has been held as truth; only art creates new truths.

I Say No (1884) reveals perhaps the weakest plotting, though the action is achieved with perhaps the greatest contrivance, of any of the novels of the last years. Emily Brown, a young woman about to finish her education and take a position as secretary in a remote place in the North, first accepts the likelihood that her father, James, died of natural causes, then begins to suspect murder, and finally discovers, by the retrieval of a lost letter, that he committed suicide. *The Evil Genius* (1886), Collins' next novel, displays at least in its narrative a somewhat greater potential, but this is rarely actualized. What might have been a work seriously concerned with the moral problem remains merely an account of the involvement of a woman in the lives of others: Mrs. Presty, the titular character, trying to impose solutions upon the collapsing marriage of Herbert and Catherine Linley, her son-in-law and daughter, is not so much "the evil genius" by the action she initiates as by her ability to turn bad situations initiated by others to utter disaster.

The Legacy of Cain (1889), the last novel which Collins was to complete, stands as his only incursion into the waters troubled by the publication of *On the Origin of Species* thirty years earlier. Concerned with what has been called "Darwinisticism" rather than with what is more properly Darwinism—that is, with notions but indirectly derived from the *Origin*[7]—*The Legacy of Cain* embodies, in a plot badly conceived and weakly sustained, the unhappy evidence of Collins' confusion about the implications of propositions concerning evolution. For those who would read only at the level of narrative, the theme of the Cain-Abel conflict, recognizable in the rivalry of the Gracedieu sisters for the love of Philip Dunboyne, would hardly be disturbing. That Helena, the blood daughter of the evangelical minister, turns out to be evil, while Eunice, an executed murderess' daughter who has been brought up by Mr. Gracedieu as his own, is virtuous, only demonstrates the fallacy of the doctrine of inherent evil, which was generally obnoxious to the social philosophy of the middle class.

Otherwise, assuming a transparently allegorical structure, *The Legacy of Cain* explores the implications about Nature's savagery —especially as it is manifested in man—in the dialogue between the Doctor and the Governor of the prison where Eunice's mother was executed, with Mr. Gracedieu in his faith and charity standing in judgment between them. For the Doctor, "the legacy of Cain" becomes, in effect, a metaphor—a way of imaging Nature's tooth-and-claw. "For twenty years past . . . I have found vices and diseases descending more frequently to children than virtue and health," he remarks to the Governor.

I don't stop to ask why: there is no end to that sort of curiosity. What I have observed is what I tell you; no more and no less. You will say this is a horribly discouraging result of experience, for it tends to show that children come into the world at a disadvantage on the day of their birth. Of course they do. Children are born deformed; children are born deaf, dumb, or blind; children are born with the seeds in them of deadly diseases. Who can account for the cruelties of creation? Why are we endowed with life—only to end in death? And does it ever strike you, when you are cutting your mutton at dinner, and your cat is catching its mouse, and your spider is suffocating its fly, that we are all, big and little together, born to one certain inheritance —the privilege of eating each other? (Chapter VI)

As principal narrator, the Governor begins the story with great uncertainty about the outcome of Mr. Gracedieu's experiment. "On his own showing (as it appeared to me), there would be two forces in a state of conflict in the child's nature as she grew up— inherited evil against inculcated good," he recalls. "Try as I might, I failed to feel the Minister's comforting conviction as to which of the two would win" (Chapter VIII). Nevertheless, the Governor's faith rests in a benign universe, so that, unlike the Doctor, he does not so much regard "the legacy of Cain" as a metaphor as he considers it an untruth. "That we, who inhabit this little planet, may be the doomed creatures of fatality, from the cradle to the grave, I am not prepared to dispute," he remarks. "But I absolutely refuse to believe that it is a fatality with no higher origin than can be found in our accidental obligation to our fathers and mothers" (Chapter XL).

In effect, it is once more the scientist who holds generally for "the legacy of Cain," arguing for a kind of determinism by which man, situated in deadly conflict with other living beings, can hardly afford the moral identity to which he aspires. But the humanitarian, the product of centuries of cultural development, holds for man's control, despite his animal roots, over his environment and the forces that would keep him from morality; ultimately—and actually shown, in the deterioration of Helena somewhat more than in the moral perseverance of Eunice—the Governor finds empirical grounds for the position he has emotionally supported.

And Mr. Gracedieu, who has assumed the role of Everyman in the allegory, finds moral vindication in the only way that, for the

Governor, would have meaning in man's continual defiance of "the legacy of Cain": "And where (some persons might say) was the poor Minister's reward for the act of mercy which had saved Eunice in her infancy? Where it ought to be! A man who worthily performs a good action finds his reward in the action itself" (Chapter LXIII).

By August, 1889, Wilkie Collins had written eighteen weekly installments of *Blind Love,* which had been appearing in *The Illustrated London News* since early July, when he requested Walter Besant to finish the novel for him. Besant took up what in book form is the first forty-five chapters, and he wrote nineteen more and an Epilogue. Collins died on September 23, but the novel continued to run its course in the *News,* until it ended in December. It was published by Chatto and Windus the following year.

Of rather more complex plot than some of Collins' recent novels, *Blind Love* somewhat persuasively reveals the moral deterioration of Iris Henley caused by her "blind love" for the wild Lord Harry Norland, an Irish rogue and quasi-patriot. After a period of marriage and financial crisis, Lord Harry becomes involved in a scheme to collect the life insurance he has taken out upon himself by substituting a consumptive victim of murder for himself. Only after Iris realizes the nature of the plot and the degree to which she has been compromised does she leave Lord Harry, and the course of her deterioration is reversed. Harry is killed by his Irish enemies, and Iris, morally rejuvenated, marries Hugh Mountjoy, who, through her tribulation, has remained faithfully near her, committed to his own "blind love." Despite its superiority in sustained narrative and characterization to a number of the novels preceding it, *Blind Love* remains at best a faint shadow of Collins' earlier achievement.

III   *Other Works, 1870–89*

Of the six novelettes which Collins published during his final years, four can lay some claim to literary merit, and then unevenly. Of these probably the weakest is *The Frozen Deep* (1874), an adaptation of the drama of 1857 and 1866. The story is strikingly simple: Richard Wardour, replaced in the affections of Clara Burnham by an unknown man, vows revenge; on an Arctic expedition, Wardour learns that Clara's fiancé is one of his peers, Francis Aldersley, with whom, by accident, Wardour is separated from the rest of the group. He now has the power to attain revenge, but, undergoing a spiritual transformation, he leads Aldersley back to civilization—and to Clara—where, his expiation fulfilled, Wardour dies in exhaustion. One of Collins' most melodramatic accomplishments, *The Frozen Deep* is also one of his most celebrated—a fact which impinges upon any attempt to make a literary judgment of it. By any standard the work is deficient: the plot is hopelessly contrived, resting entirely upon a major coincidence, and the central character's principal decision, on which the only significant action turns, is incredibly motivated. Yet these conclusions may be obscured, or at least assimilated, by the image handed down through book and tradition of the play's production at Tavistock House in 1857, with Dickens' performance as Richard Wardour, passionate but exhausted, to Wilkie Collins' Francis Aldersley.

Miss or Mrs? (1873) has no tradition of dramatic performance either to confuse judgments of its literary merits or to emphasize its absurdities. At the center of the story stands Richard Turlington, a highly successful merchant of early middle age and, it is firmly suggested, of dubious past. As suitor to Natalie Graybrooke, daughter of the incredibly wealthy Sir Joseph, Turlington hesitates at nothing to bring the girl, with her wealth, to an early marriage; when he realizes that his schemes have been checked, he becomes savage in a way that is unparalleled in Collins' work, firing a pistol through a door in an effort to kill Sir Joseph. Unlike most of Collins' villains, Richard Turlington has in his past life only darkness, nothing to explain or mitigate the evil that is his. He becomes totally sinister, and with his absolute villainy binds together the elements of what in all other respects is an extraordinarily weak piece of fiction.

In *John Jago's Ghost* (1873–74) the achievement is somewhat more remarkable, resting upon a greater variety of characters, generally well motivated and integrated with their stark rural American background. Based upon a legal episode which had occurred in Vermont in 1819,[8] Collins' novelette uses the theme of the presumed dead returning to life. Found in earlier works, most strikingly in *Sister Rose* and "The Dead Hand," it was here put to credible use in the case of John Jago, for whose supposed murder the Meadowcroft brothers are convicted on the basis of massive circumstantial evidence. Only after the young men have been

sentenced to death is Jago, who has fled the Meadowcroft farm
in bitterness and anger, induced to return and then captured.

Aiding credibility and imposing a cohesiveness upon the narrative elements is the very mood permeating the farmhouse and all
its world, from which only two beings are exempt, and they are
the least compelling characters in the novelette: Philip Lefrank, a
visiting Englishman, the narrator trying to impose a somewhat
objective order on what he relates; Naomi Colebrook, the or-
phaned cousin of the Meadowcrofts, bright amidst their darkness.
All else is the stark Puritan American setting, with its social suppression and personal frustration, in which brother betrays
brother and the living are committed to the endurance until death
of life's work and pain.

Miss Meadowcroft, the daughter of the invalid farmer Isaac
Meadowcroft, though clearly an extreme instance, is representative of the spirit creating the atmosphere at the farm: "She was a
melancholy, middle-aged woman, without visible attractions of
any sort—one of those persons who appear to accept the obligation of living under protest, as a burden which they never would
have consented to bear if they had only been consulted first"
(Chapter II). If Collins essentially misinterpreted his American
materials,[9] he used them with extraordinary skill to create an
atmosphere that permeates and sustains the narrative.

Countering those who insist upon a steady decline in Collins'
abilities is the fact that for its kind *The Haunted Hotel: A Mystery
of Modern Venice* (1879) was one of his most successful under-
takings. The question may arise about the worth of the *kind* itself,
the sensation narrative, of which this is an almost pure example.
With a highly complex and to no purpose plot—contrived around
mysterious experiments, secrets from the past, the substitution of
one man for another in death, and the shadowy barrier between
sanity and madness—*The Haunted Hotel* moves toward one cli-
mactic scene, in which all the possibilities of sensation are realized. Agnes Lockwood, the female protagonist, awakens in the
haunted room to find the evil Countess Narona sitting in a stupor
beside her; "midway between her [own] face and the ceiling"
hovers "a human head—severed at the neck, like a head struck
from the body by a guillotine." Agnes, captured by the terror of
the apparition, sees nothing else:

The flesh of the face was gone. The shriveled skin was darkened in hue, like the skin of an Egyptian mummy—except at the neck. There it was of a lighter color; there it showed spots and splashes of the hue of that brown spot on the ceiling, which the child's fanciful terror had distorted into the likeness of a spot of blood. Thin remains of a discolored mustache and whiskers, hanging over the upper lip, and over the hollows where the cheeks had once been, made the head just recognizable as the head of a man. Over all the features death and time had done their obliterating work. The eyelids were closed. The hair on the skull, discolored like the hair on the face, had been burned away in places. The bluish lips, parted in a fixed grin, showed the double row of teeth. By slow degrees, the hovering head (perfectly still when she first saw it) began to descend toward Agnes as she lay beneath. By slow degrees, that strange doubly-blended odor, which the Commissioners had discovered in the vaults of the old palace—which had sickened Francis Westwick in the bed-chamber of the new hotel—spread its fetid exhalations over the room. Downward and downward the hideous apparition made its slow progress, until it stopped close over Agnes—stopped, and turned slowly, so that the face of it confronted the upturned face of the woman in the chair. (Chapter XXII)

Mitigating the purity of this novelette as sensation fiction is the moral conflict that is taking place in the mind of Countess Narona, who sees herself compelled by fate to commit acts of evil and thereby bring on her own destruction. Thus she assimilates the fatality of the story into her own motivation, causing the incidents that would otherwise be considered fatal; as T. S. Eliot emphasized, the melodramatic therefore becomes a quality of her character rather than of the work itself in which that character occurs.[10]

In the last years Collins wrote some short stories, but few of significance. "The Fatal Fortune" (1874) is a more pointed attack upon the system of private asylums and their abuse by the unscrupulous than Collins had made in *The Woman in White*; here, painfully illustrating the most striking fault others were to find with his fiction of social criticism, he concluded with a frank statement of the "moral" of his story: "Assisted by a doctor, whose honesty and capacity must be taken on trust, these interested persons [the covetous relatives of a wealthy Englishman], in this nineteenth century of progress, can lawfully imprison their relative for life, in a country which calls itself free, and which declares that its justice is equally administered to all alike."

In 1887 Chatto and Windus published fourteen short stories in three volumes under the title *Little Novels*. Collected from Collins' periodical publication during the 1870's and the first half of the 1880's, these were retitled so that each bears the name of two characters, such as "Mrs. Zant and the Ghost" or "Miss Mina and the Groom." Contrived in their plots and in their happy conclusions, they illustrate nothing so much as the degree to which Collins was unevenly losing control of his materials; in each story there are perhaps several of the characteristics marking the earlier and finer work, but in none of these was the informing spirit active.

The final plays were largely adaptations of the novels. *The Woman in White* opened at the Olympic Theatre on October 9, 1871, and ran for nineteen weeks. *Man and Wife* began a run of twenty-three weeks on February 22, 1873, at the Prince of Wales's Theatre. Several months later, on May 19, *The New Magdalen* opened at the Olympic, to run for nineteen weeks before it was taken on a provincial tour. *Miss Gwilt*, an adaptation of *Armadale*, produced in Liverpool in December, 1875, was at the Globe Theatre for twelve weeks beginning in April, 1876. *The Moonstone* lasted for nine weeks at the Olympic, from September 17, 1877. An original drama, *Rank and Riches*, passed one week at the Adelphi in June, 1883. And in 1885 there was a single performance, for copyright purposes, of *The Evil Genius*.

CHAPTER 7

The World of Wilkie Collins

I Collins and His Century

WILKIE COLLINS was a representative product of the nine-teenth-century literary situation. Well before his middle years he assumed the role of popular novelist—a role which had gradually emerged in the late eighteenth century, to be filled and shaped by Walter Scott and Benjamin Disraeli—with the responsibilities that it imposed upon him in his relation to the ever-growing and frequently voracious reading public. Principal among these was the happy ending, reassuring the reader that virtue is, after all, rewarded, just as vice is finally punished. With contrivance that occasionally stimulates wonder, Collins managed to impose such conclusions upon all of his novels, every novelette except *The Dream Woman,* and more than half of the short stories. Because of his success in meeting this responsibility, critics of several generations as well as his readers have assumed his faith in the ethos of the middle-class Victorian public. Consequently, his relation to other aspects of his time, particularly in his awareness and expression of the intellectual currents of Victorian England, has to a large degree been eclipsed.

The measure of such a relation is difficult to attain, particularly for one whose personal life remained intentionally obscure, most of whose friends recording their recollections were largely concerned with his achievements in the theater or the literary market place, and from whom but few surviving letters are known. Wilkie Collins was certainly not, in the ordinary sense, an intellectual; yet throughout his life he was associated with men who, in the practice of their professions or their arts, were keenly aware of the currents passing about them.

No one sets out consciously to be a man of his own time, a "Renaissance man" or a "Victorian man," but every man of intelligence and sensitivity reflects what is thought and written and read around him, refined or confused though it may be when it is assimilated into the conscious and subconscious levels of his mind. Wilkie Collins was clearly no exception. His mature and creative years began approximately in 1850, the year of the publication of the Victorians' most plaintiff cry for faith in Tennyson's *In Memoriam*; and his life ended the year following the publication of Mrs. Humphry Ward's *Robert Elsmere*, the first novel to put before the public the controversy over the supernatural assumptions of religion. Contemporaneity in itself does not constitute susceptibility to the influences of an age, but, in examining a case like Collins', knowledge of it will add to the perspective needed for an evaluation of what lies beneath the surface of the narratives. Though Collins' world view is neither so refined as Matthew Arnold's nor so independent of traditional assumptions as Thomas Henry Huxley's, it is far removed from that of most of the reading public for whom he wrote.

In Collins' writings there is very little reference to the intellectual currents of his own time, or even to their cultural ramifications; what does appear frequently suggests a confusion in both comprehension and attitude. From *The Legacy of Cain* it seems that Collins' essential misunderstanding of the Darwinian impact was compounded by his deep dislike of what he regarded as an affront to man's moral identity, to human dignity itself. In *The Law and the Lady*, old Benjamin, who in other respects seems to serve as a spokeman for Collins, strikes forth, vehemently if somewhat comically, at the apparent cause for the collapse of order in his own times:

"Oh, the new ideas! the new ideas! By all manner of means, Valeria, let us have the new ideas! The old morality's all wrong, the old ways are all worn out. Let's march with the age we live in. Nothing comes amiss to the age we live in. . . . . Let's go and get crammed with ready-made science at a lecture—let's hear the last new professor, the man who has been behind the scenes at Creation, and knows to a T how the world was made, and how long it took to make it. There's the other fellow, too: mind we don't forget the modern Solomon, who has left his proverbs behind him—the brand-new philosopher who considers the consolations of religion in the light of harmless playthings, and who is kind enough to say that he might have been all the happier if he could only have been childish enough to play with them himself. Oh, the new ideas! the new ideas!—what consoling, elevating, beautiful discoveries have been made by the new ideas! We were all monkeys before we were men, and molecules before we were monkeys! And what does it matter? And what does any thing matter to any body?" (Chapter XXXIX)

Benjamin's beliefs should not be literally equated to those of Collins, if for no other reason than because Collins rejected the supernaturalism of Christianity; not in the apparent opposition to evolutionary hypothesis but in the evident confusion to which the implication of this hypothesis has led the old man does he speak for Collins and for a large number of the intellectually acute of his generation. It was neither in defense of the old ideas nor in commitment to the new, but in the bewilderment preceding commitment that the major writers of the nineteenth century expressed their reaction to the ontological conflict going on about them. The literature that they produced was primarily one of alienation and only thereafter one of affirmation or negation.

Characteristically, the protagonist first accepts a view of reality, an orientation, which, in the light of a given experience, he suddenly finds inadequate, so that he moves into a phase of profound disorientation, marked by an awareness of his own alienation from the standards and comforts of those around him. Although he can never simply re-enter the society to which he once belonged, he may be able, by constructing a new set of values from the experience that he has had, to understand it. The Victorian literature of alienation is most clearly represented by Matthew Arnold; the literature of the full value-process, moving from orientation through alienation to reorientation itself, is practically legion: Carlyle's *Sartor Resartus* (1833–34), Tennyson's *In Memoriam*, Newman's *Apologia Pro Vita Sua* (1864), and John Stuart Mill's *Autobiography* (1873), to mention the most striking examples.

From the beginning Collins' work is marked by examples of alienation, though, like Sarah Leeson (*The Dead Secret*), his aliens may be among his most unintelligent characters, and certainly not all attain self-awareness. Particularly in the early novels, a character may stand between two cultures, belonging to neither: Ulpius (*Antonina*), a votary to the dead gods in living Rome, or Hermanric, despised by his own Goths and yet no Roman; Basil, caught between the sociocultural world of his father and that of Mr. Sherwin, and Mannion, his face bearing the marks of Basil's wrath, explicitly likened to Cain's descendant; Mat Marksman (*Hide and Seek*), alien in his own land and yet never really part of North America.

On occasion alienation results from guilt, which a character may come to understand: Mr. Thorpe (*Hide and Seek*) carries such a burden but not so well as Mrs. Catherick (*The Woman in White*); Ozias Midwinter (*Armadale*) bears guilt for his father; Hester Dethridge (*Man and Wife*) and Mercy Merrick (*The New Magdalen*) have been alienated from society by acts to which the conditions of society drove them; Eustace Macallan (*The Law and the Lady*) bears the mark in society of a guilt that is not really his; and Franklin Blake (*The Moonstone*) cannot at first comprehend the way in which he is guilty.

Alienation of some type may also derive from a responsibility thrust upon a character: Sarah Leeson striving to fulfill the demands of her pledge and Alfred Monkton to avoid the effects of the family curse; Gabriel moving to total alienation when his simplistic orientation fails to sustain the shock from the situation created by his father; Ida Welwyn, in her isolated existence at Glenwith Grange, carrying the emotional burden imposed upon her by her sister's tragedy.

The most acute form of alienation is, however, that of one who is living but presumed dead, of which the case of Laura Fairlie is most memorable. "Torn in her own lifetime from the list of the living, the daughter of Philip Fairlie and the wife of Percival Glyde might still exist for her sister, might still exist for me, but to all the world besides she was dead," Hartright remarks. "Dead to her uncle, who had renounced her; dead to the servants of the house, who had failed to recognise her; dead to the persons in authority who had transmitted her fortune to her husband and her aunt; dead to my mother and my sister, who believed me to be the dupe of an adventuress and the victim of a fraud; socially, morally, legally—dead" (*The Woman in White*, Third Epoch. Walter Hartright's Narrative, II).

And, for Collins as for Dickens,[1] the city, especially London, may be both the ultimate phase and the clearest symbol of modern man's alienation; here, men exist totally reduced to their roles and deprived of all identity, unknown to each other and perhaps to themselves:

Observant persons, accustomed to frequent the London parks, can hardly have failed to notice the number of solitary strangers sadly endeavoring to vary their lives by taking a walk. They linger about the flower beds; they sit for hours on the benches; they look with patient curiosity at other people who have companions; they notice ladies on horseback and children at play with submissive interest; some of the men find company in a pipe, without appearing to enjoy it; some of the women find a substitute for dinner in little dry biscuits wrapped in crumpled scraps of paper; they are not sociable; they are hardly ever seen to make acquaintance with each other; perhaps they are shamefaced, or proud, or sullen; perhaps they despair of others, being accustomed to despair of themselves; perhaps they have their reasons for never venturing to encounter curiosity, or their vices which dread detection, or their virtues which suffer hardship with the resignation that is sufficient for itself. The one thing certain is, that these unfortunate people resist discovery. We know that they are strangers in London, and we know no more (*I Say No*, Chapter XXI).

Striking among Collins' characters is the number of those who are in some way afflicted so that they are set off from other beings. Madonna (*Hide and Seek*) is deaf and dumb; Leonard Frankland (*The Dead Secret*) is blind, as is Lucilla Finch (*Poor Miss Finch*); Frederick Fairlie is reduced to the mercy of his own hypochondria, and Miserrimus Dexter (*The Law and the Lady*) to his wheel chair and his delusions. Oscar Dubourg (*Poor Miss Finch*) is, of course, set off by his appearance. In each instance, while the affliction furthers plot, at times crucially, it also sets up a situation symbolizing, particularly in the modern context, one aspect of the human condition.

Although in some cases, such as Frederick Fairlie's, the afflicted learns nothing from his isolation or becomes, like Miserrimus Dexter in his solipsistic universe, the ultimate alien, frequently those who are so set off establish for themselves the means by which life can be made purposeful. Of Madonna, the narrator remarks: "Exiled alike from the worlds of sound and speech, the poor girl's enjoyment of all that she could still gain of happiness, by means of the seeing sense that was left her, was hardly conceivable to her speaking and hearing fellow-creatures" (*Hide and Seek*, Book I, Chapter VII). For the traditionally oriented among Collins' readers, Madonna's experience is *adaptation*; for others who, like a number of nineteenth-century thinkers, found little outside the self to which to adapt, it is reorientation, the creation of a new world of values out of private experience.

A more direct means used by Collins to convey the quality of alienation is by the image of insanity or sometimes amentia. In some of his narratives Collins made no distinction between intellectual derangement and incapacity, though the afflicted persons may be divisible by another standard. There are those whose insanity results more or less directly from extreme disorientation: the malefactors Ulpius and Goisvintha (*Antonina*); to some extent, Sarah Leeson; and certainly, Hester Dethridge. There are also those who in their mental alienation—often as significantly marked by incapacity as by derangement—impose order upon what takes place around them and remain, paradoxically, the silent embodiments of meaning in an otherwise mad world: again, Sarah Leeson; Mrs. Wragge (*No Name*) is disordered amid the committedly immoral world of her husband; Jack Frost (*Jezebel's Daughter*), with something less than reason, ultimately comprehends the nightmare world of Madame Fontaine; and Mrs. Sherwin (*Basil*) appears insane because her orderly orientation recurringly collapses when it faces the chaos in which she must live.

Collins' aliens, vividly and significantly developed as characters, usually do not pass to reorientation. There are exceptions, of course; Franklin Blake's very assembling of the documents reconstructing the episode of the Moonstone is the means by which, once alienated not only from others but from his own sense of self as well, he is able to confirm his own reorientation. More frequently, reorientation is mythically cast as expiation, which—though at one level it may be seen as continually adding new dimensions to itself and to one's perspective—assumes a reality outside of the self to which one has to conform. Numerian's "existence was one vast sacrifice, one scene of intrepid self-immolation" (*Antonina,* Chapter IV). Mr. Thorpe is committed to religious societies; Ozias Midwinter, to self-sacrifice for Allan Armadale; Lewis Romayne (*The Black Robe*), to the priesthood; Gabriel's father, to the restoration of roadside crosses; and both Richard Wardour (*The Frozen Deep*) and Nugent Dubourg, to the barren silence of an Arctic expedition. Basil purges himself by writing the record of his folly and its consequences; Sara Macallan, the story of her own jealous love and blighted marriage; and the Countess Narona (*The Haunted Hotel*), the drama memorializing her own evil. Mercy Merrick, one of Collins' most intensely expiational characters, who must periodically repeat the story of "The purgatory on earth of her past life" (*The New Magdalen*, Chapter XXVI), becomes a nurse during the Franco-Prussian War, illustrating the observation of Madame Pratolungo: "Modern despair turns nurse, binds up wounds, gives physic, and gets cured or not in that useful but nasty way" (*Poor Miss Finch*, Chapter XLVI).

II *Villainy, Major and Minor*

Throughout Collins' novels appear certain characters who, though not passing into philosophic disorientation, find themselves so ill-adapted, either because of guilt or circumstances, to the world in which they must live that in compensation they insistently seek to impose their view of life upon that world and all who enter it. They regard the structure of outer reality as rigid and their own relation to it as authoritarian. This type of character, which might be called a *negative absolutist*,[2] occurs increasingly in modern literature, and is a reflection of Western man's growing (and terrifying) incertitude during the last several centuries. The expression of such absolutism may take any of a number of forms.

In Collins' works it is occasionally political, as in the case of Danville (*Sister Rose*); or social, as with Mrs. Catherick; but more frequently it is moral or religious. The righteous Miss Joanna Grice (*Hide and Seek*) takes the "sin" of her niece as a personal offense against herself; her concept of morality is totally egocentric. Similarly, Mrs. Milroy (*Armadale*), deep in the surety of her own morality, suspects no inconsistency in herself in using the most evil instruments against the evil Miss Gwilt. Mrs. Lecount (*No Name*), protecting Noel Vanstone, and Grace Roseberry (*The New Magdalen*), seeking recognition of her rightful identity, are somewhat more ambiguous cases; for, though appearing within the context of the respective action as negative absolutists, each is defending what by the established standards of her society is hers.

The religiously oriented negative absolutists are in no sense hypocrites, irrespective of the inconsistencies that their behavior may appear to have within a larger orientation. Mr. Thorpe sincerely repents of the sins secretly recalled from his own past and finds absolution in present piety. Mr. Finch cannot recognize the canting absurdity in his own behavior. Certainly, Miss Meadowcroft (*John Jago's Ghost*) believes sincerely in the moral reality of her stark image of Providence.

The most striking instance is Druscilla Clack, continually adjusting her moral responses to existing circumstances without any sense of her own accommodation. Her good must thrive upon the evil she finds in others. In many ways a heavily drawn portrait of a socially and sexually deprived woman turning in compensation to the evangelical redemption of the world, Druscilla Clack is in no sense a caricature. She has lost all capacity to make distinctions —between her humility and her pride in that humility, between her will to save others' souls and their own power of resistance to her efforts, between her very record of events and the events themselves, between pleasure and pain, and finally between herself and the world. There is for Druscilla Clack no reality beyond her own emotional strivings, which she projects as "the holy inner voice that never deceives," directing the Christian to his acts of truth:

> Once self-supported by conscience, once embarked on a career of manifest usefulness, the true Christian never yields. Neither public nor private influences produce the slightest effect on us, when we have once got our mission. Taxation may be the consequence of a mission; riots may be the consequence of a mission; wars may be the consequence of a mission: we go on with our work, irrespective of every human consideration which moves the world outside us. We are above reason; we are beyond ridicule; we see with nobody's eyes, we hear with nobody's ears, we feel with nobody's hearts but our own. Glorious, glorious privilege! And how is it earned? Ah, my friends, you may spare yourselves the useless inquiry! We are the only people who can earn it—for we are the only people who are always right.
>
> (*The Moonstone*, Druscilla Clack's Narrative, Chapter IV)

It is hardly surprising that at the end of her narrative, repudiated by those around her, left alone in the room at Verinder's, Druscilla paradoxically attains the fulfillment of her messianic impulses, recording her situation as "this touching picture of a Christian persecuted by the world" (Chapter VII).

Most significantly, Druscilla Clack fails to distinguish between herself and her own image of deity; all that she regards as desirable in her own world she necessarily attributes to God. Though she masks this confusion from herself, as well as from others, in her role of religious commitment, she, imposing her will upon those around her, is not unlike a number of Collins' characters who, more overtly villainous than Druscilla, assume the role of deity in their own small worlds. Though negative absolutism in itself is only self-deceiving and therefore does not partake of conscious villainy, it well may lead to and express villainy.

In Collins' works one seems to become a villain at that point that he begins *consciously* to try to exploit the wills of others, to manipulate their lives. Count Fosco (*The Woman in White*) is the supreme instance, reflected by a host of others: John Jago, through his feigned death, attempts to play the lives of men against each other; Baron Rivar (*The Haunted Hotel*) and Lord Harry Norland (*Blind Love*) assume the right, traditionally attributed to divinity, to preside over the distinction between life and death; Miserrimus Dexter tries to control others' wills by indirect devices as he controls Ariel's by direct means; Dr. Benjulia (*Heart and Science*), with his surgical instruments, moves as if anointed through the world of men and animals to determine which of them might live.

Benjulia more directly illustrates a failure implied in others: he cannot distinguish between man and animal; therefore, he asserts neither the potential dignity of the one nor the latent savagery of the other. Several of the negative absolutists of villainous proportions in Collins' works are lovers of animals, providing with tenderness over the worlds of the small creatures while they simultaneously range for predatory purposes through the worlds of men. Again, no case is more striking than that of Fosco, whose birds and mice constitute the only benign microcosm to which he can make commitment. Margaret Sherwin has a canary with which she plays, gently coaxing and teasing, much as she plays with Basil himself.

And Mrs. Lecount, presiding over the death-fringed world of Noel Vanstone, keeps a toad—"solitary, cold as the stone, brown as the stone, motionless as the stone" on which he sits (*No Name*, Scene III, Chapter II)—as the hideous mark of the power that is hers. The creature is only too suggestive of the invalid and neurotic Noel, who sits, not quite so silently, as the other symbol of Mrs. Lecount's power. Indeed, Noel himself would assume the role of a deity, manipulating the wills and lives of others, but in his shadow world he has not the power—and the animals that he possesses are all stuffed.

What essentially constitutes the conscious exploitation or manipulation that is villainy? When, if ever, does Druscilla Clack, bent on converting mankind, begin to conquer it? The question is difficult. So long as Druscilla remains ineffective, her will to convert, rather than merely to project upon those around her the dimensions of her own necrophilic being, is not established; possibly, success would destroy Druscilla, for then there would be no "evil" for her to hate; by the process of exclusion, she would have no choice but to love. But, assuming Druscilla's commitment to affect the lives and wills of others, we can argue only that she becomes villainous when she succeeds in doing so. Although the abandonment of the moral intention (which may lead first to amorality, then to immorality) seems to be a constituent of villainy in Collins' world, the measure of villainy is at the surface of interpersonal relations. It is a world in which, largely, men create and judge their own morality.

Despite the fact that nearly all the narratives conclude with the triumphant happiness of the virtuous, the line between good and evil in the world of Collins' novels is neither firm nor straight. David Glenney, as narrator in one part of *Jezebel's Daughter*, describes the correspondence of Madame Fontaine, which he has just presented, "as a picture of a perverted mind, struggling between good and evil, and slowly losing ground under the stealthy influence of temptation" (Chapter XV). Evaluating the motives and actions of Misserimus Dexter, the attorney Mr. Playmore, a spokesman to be trusted in *The Law and the Lady*, concludes: "There are degrees in all wickedness. Dexter was wicked enough to suppress the letter, which wounded his vanity . . . but he was not wicked enough deliberately to let an innocent man perish on the scaffold" (Chapter XLIX). And in *The Black Robe*, the narrator proposes that, "When you want to see unredeemed wickedness, look for it in a fool" (Book V, Chapter IV). Whatever good may be (and, for the most part, Collins does not make clear what qualities it possesses), evil in the world of Collins' novels is far from absolute—it is a condition brought forth by time and circumstance, and it is occasionally mixed even with good.

Since, with but few exceptions, Collins' novels and shorter narratives center upon conflict which appears to concern the forces of good and evil, the villain is structurally far more important than the presumed hero, who frequently may be only a rather passive protagonist. It is the villain who preys upon the good (often so innocent as to be defenseless), who creates the conflict and sustains the central situation. Though in the Western theological tradition, evil is defined as existing only in the absence of good, for Wilkie Collins in the world of his novels, as for many of his literary contemporaries, good is effective only in the absence of evil. Despite their importance, however, the villains in Collins' narratives are thoroughly corrupt in only a few instances; Richard Turlington (*Miss or Mrs?*), appearing to be intrinsically evil and without redemptive possibility, may be the most remarkable. To the mass of Collins' readers, who were for the most part committed to the two-valued moral orientation, the inconsistency in villainy seems not to have been obnoxious so long as the endings of the narratives displayed the triumph of virtue.

Most of Collins' supposed villains have been corrupted by the treatment life has accorded them. Goisvintha and Ulpius are examples, each of whom has been deprived of identity and purpose by enemy hordes. Even Mannion, humorless and resolute, is a victim of his past life. Sir Percival Glyde is a bastard son, and Miserrimus Dexter is born with incredibly horrible afflictions. Lydia Gwilt was an outcast, as was Mercy Merrick (whose villainy is really transformed into a variety of sentimental heroism). Some presumed villains are doubtfully guilty: Mr. Thorpe is largely swept up by circumstances, and Nugent Dubourg becomes a victim of his own uncontrollable passion for Lucilla Finch. Not surprisingly, villains possess at least some socially redeeming characteristics. Again, Fosco, ultimately one of the most clearly dangerous personalities, becomes the primary example: learned, quiet, apparently tolerant, and a lover of animals, he is as appealing to those around him as to the readers of 1860. Lydia Gwilt is partially redeemed by her own love for Ozias Midwinter, and Captain Wragge moves gradually from the sinister to the comic.

There is in Collins' fictional world nothing so revealing as the vicarious punishments imposed upon his supposed villains. Even Richard Turlington dies by the accidental discharge of his own revolver. The device obviously relieves protagonists of the burden of pain or the mark of blood for inflicting what appears to be deserved. But, more than this, within the context of a kind of moral accounting, it seems, even to the superficial reader of—say —1865, to give what in all ways is expected without going beyond the bounds of order or balance. From the beginning, vicarious retribution appears in Collins' works. Ulpius kills Goisvintha and then is himself sacrificed by the priests. Margaret Sherwin dies of typhus, and Mannion falls from Cornish rocks into the sea. Mr. Thorpe dies of natural causes intensified by the shock of being discovered. Sir Percival Glyde perishes in a fire that is really of his own origin, and Count Fosco at the hands of the anonymous members of a secret society. Godfrey Ablewhite (*The Moonstone*) is murdered by three equally anonymous Indians, and Geoffrey Delamayn (*Man and Wife*) by the maddened Hester Dethridge. Nugent Dubourg is lost in an Arctic expedition. Lydia Gwilt destroys herself knowingly, and Madame Fontaine unknowingly. Danville dies in a duel, Father Rocco (*The Yellow Mask*) is mysteriously sent to Rome, and Dr. Benjulia goes mad.

III   A World of God and Man

Nothing so much illustrates the moral context of the world of Collins' novels as the place occupied by religion and its spokesmen—and nothing is so easily misunderstood.[3] Though the influence of the Church (or of the Protestant chapel) had waned by the mid-nineteenth century, the society in which Collins lived was far less secular than that of the twentieth century, and judgment of the Church and its spokesmen was a principal criterion by which the individual himself was judged.

Clerics, who abound in Collins' works, hold the positions of pseudoprotagonists, villains, even fools; they are to be judged not so much by what they do as by the larger context in which they do it. Those of extremely Protestant orientations, committed to a notion of duty or to an abstract sense of right and wrong, though not villains, generally make difficulties for themselves and those they love; Mr. Carling ("The Parson's Scruple") leaves his wife and dies soon thereafter when he learns that she has been divorced. The Reverend Danbury Daker, rector of Tidbury-on-the-Marsh, one of presumed Low Church commitment, is described by a local Squire, who speaks somewhat with authorial sanction, as "a canting sneak—a sort of fellow who goes into poor people's cottages, asking what they've got for dinner, and when they tell him, he takes the cover off the saucepan and sniffs at it, to make sure that they've spoken the truth" (*Mr. Wray's Cash-Box,* Chapter VI).

Mr. Finch, an Anglican of similar orientation, deprived of recognition in the larger world, demands it of the smaller, where he confuses his own will with that of "all wise Providence" and assumes the role of vengeful deity in pronouncing judgments upon the meaning of the blindness of his daughter Lucilla. Counterpoised are Dr. Joyce (*Hide and Seek*), who combines his offices as cleric and as magistrate to effect the good, and Mr. Gracedieu (*The Legacy of Cain*), known merely as "the Minister" but presumably not committed to the High Church. Julian Gray (*The New Magdalen*), an Anglican of aristocratic stamp, is a singular instance of the truly committed Christian priest, but then Gray hardly survives in his own priesthood.

The Roman Catholic Father Benwell (*The Black Robe*) is an obvious extension of Father Rocco, determined and perhaps cruel, but only within the scope of his motivation to aid the Church. Vindicating the Roman clergy stand Father Arthur Penrose (*The Black Robe*), also a Jesuit, and eminently Father Paul (*Gabriel's Marriage*), the unflinching priest who brings hope to the Breton peasants during the French Terror.

Collins made few comments in his writings about the value of organized religion, but these bear out the implications of the behavior of his clerical characters. Arguing in *Rambles Beyond Railways* (1852) that the diminution of religious ritual has deprived modern man of much of the significant fusion of natural beauty and religious beauty, Collins in no way defended the social or private ethic derived from imposing a literal construction upon the substance of ritual. In the section of this book entitled "The Nuns of Mawgan," he proposed that the value of the cloistered life cannot even be estimated by men committed to the secular world: "It is not for us, guided only by our own thoughts, moved only by the impulses of the world we live in, to decide upon the measure of good or evil contained in an act of self-sacrifice at the altar of religion, which is in its own motive and result so utterly separated from all other motives and results, that we cannot at the outset even so much as sympathise with it." [4]

The implications in this early book are abundantly illustrated in the narratives themselves. In no instance is the structure of the

Church—Roman, Anglican, or otherwise—or the motivation of its
members questioned so long as neither impinges upon the social
structure itself or upon the happiness and the freedom of individual human beings. Lewis Romayne's capacity to worship in solitude, in a Roman as well as in an Anglican Church, is admirable;
only when his religious drives cause him to desert and injure his
wife are they deplorable. The clerics—Benwell, Rocco, Finch,
Paul, Gracedieu, Gray—are judged in teleological terms, by what
in their actions they intend to do and to become.

But the teleological itself must have a foundation, a criterion by
which man's purpose can be measured. For Collins, as for so
many of his century and of ours, no higher truth than that derived
from man was attainable. The world is filled with good and evil,
but these are relative values, pluralistically conceived and measured by their effect upon man's interpersonal relations. Father
Rocco or Father Benwell is not evil merely because he *wills* evil
but because what he does, no matter how sincerely motivated,
works toward the disruption of operating society and of private
happiness; at the conclusion of the narrative, his damage rectified,
he is dismissed in frustration or given into the hands of the
Church for disciplining.

Human fulfillment is the measure of the highest truth and the
most compelling morality; no greater judge sits than society itself.
The world of Wilkie Collins is neither superficial nor simplified
just because it is deprived of transcendental standards. It is the
secular world of many nineteenth-century thinkers and writers[5]—
of Dickens and of Trollope and of William James—in which men,
caught between their potential and their deficiencies, are the creators and the measure of all value.

CHAPTER 8

The Achievement of Wilkie Collins: A Conclusion

I *Characters and Types*

CONCEIVED in pluralistic terms, each of Collins' characters, though not manifestly complex himself, represents the results of the interaction of complex forces.[1] Though many are simplistic in their view of the world, none is truly simple. "We all are . . . a compound of many opposite qualities possessed [of] a character with more than one side to it," observes the narrator in *Man and Wife* (Chapter XXX). To this Madame Pratolungo can add what her experience has taught her: "the narrowest human limits are wide enough to contain the grandest human emotions" (*Poor Miss Finch,* Chapter I). "Is it the good or the evil fortune of mortals that the comic side of life, and the serious side of life, are perpetually in collision with each other?" asks the Governor of the Prison in *The Legacy of Cain* (Chapter XXXV), one as reliably a Collins spokesman as Madame Pratolungo.

A quality of Collins' characters, certainly when ideally developed, is that none is entirely predictable, existing somewhat distinct from the situations in which he participates. Each character is a compound of many attributes, often discordant, which can be measured only in the social context. For this reason, though Collins argued in the Preface to *The Woman in White* for the possibility of character without plot, it is, in his world as depicted, not a likelihood. The motivation of a character must in the end be evaluated by the impact of his actions upon other human beings. Miserrimus Dexter becomes a significant being only to the extent that, from the horrors of his solipsistic world, he impinges upon the lives of others.

Many characters never attain this dynamic quality. The secondary beings who do not become significantly involved with others constitute part of a background that is essential to the full interaction among the primary characters. Using something of the paint-

er's method, selecting a quality that is both memorable and sufficient for the position that the character must assume in the scene,
Collins strove, somewhat epigrammatically, to capture the static
reality. The servant Betsey is one who "spoke on the principle of
drowning the smallest possible infusion of ideas in the largest possible dilution of words" (*The Dead Secret*, Book IV, Chapter IV).
Somewhat more abundantly and memorably presented is Laura
Fairlie's former governess:

Mrs. Vesey looked the personification of human composure and female amiability. A calm enjoyment of a calm existence beamed in
drowsy smiles on her plump, placid face. Some of us rush through
life, and some of us saunter through life. Mrs. Vesey *sat* through life.
Sat in the house, early and late; sat in the garden; sat in unexpected
window-seats in passages; sat (on a camp-stool) when her friends
tried to take her out walking; sat before she looked at any thing,
before she talked of any thing, before she answered Yes, or No, to
the commonest question—always with the same serene smile on her
lips, the same vacantly attentive turn of her head, the same snugly
comfortable position of her hands and arms, under every possible
change of domestic circumstances.

> (*The Woman in White*. First Epoch. The Story
> continued by Walter Hartright, Chapter VIII)

In *Man and Wife*, the keeper of the inn that plays so crucial a part
in the action needs for her role only one social quality: "Mistress
Inchbare was tall and thin, and decent and dry. Mistress Inchbare's unlovable hair clung fast round her head in wiry little yellow curls. Mistress Inchbare's hard bones showed themselves, like
Mistress Inchbare's hard Presbyterianism, without any conceal-
ment or compromise. In short, a savagely-respectable woman,
who plumed herself on presiding over a savagely-respectable inn"
(Chapter IX). And, finally, the long-suffering though hardly in-
spiring second wife of the Reverend Mr. Finch is described: "If
there can be such a thing as *a damp woman*, this was one. There
was a humid shine on her colorless white face, and an overflow of
water in her pale blue eyes" (*Poor Miss Finch*, Chapter III).

Otherwise, characters, including some of the minor as well as
all of the major, are seen in the context of action; judged at the
level of interpersonal relationship rather than against a static
background or in a single posture, each seems to assume, until the

end of action or the conclusion of his part, a constant *becoming* rather than a definable *being*. Collins clearly did not sympathize with the motivations of a number of characters, especially when these derived from a world view which he regarded as superstitious, but, in most instances, he was able to relate the motivation to the action itself. Furthermore, in the world of his novels, a secular and subjective world without a common body of belief and motivation, the standards of the characters themselves and their personal goals are frequently quite shallow—a condition operating within the narrative itself which is not at all the same as the shallow characterization of which Collins has on occasion been accused. Usually the characters are set off against a rather prolonged sequence of situations, many though not all of which serve to illustrate another facet of the personality. In some instances, the plot—when judged by the demands that characterization imposes upon it—is critically overcomplicated.

Perhaps nothing argues so firmly for the depth of Collins' characterization as the use to which he puts the notion of the unconscious self. Though this attains its highest expression in the resolution of the immediate mystery in *The Moonstone*, Collins showed as early as *Antonina* a concern with the effects of retrogression—in the case of Ulpius—in which the impressions of the conscious present faded into the deeper reality of the unconscious past. Mrs. Wragge, in her gigantism and stupidity, is able at least to make a distinction, which she of course does not understand, between her conscious actions and whatever causes her to behave as she does: " 'I beg your pardon, doctor, my conduct isn't ladylike, I know. It's my head, sir; it isn't *me*. I must give vent somehow, or my head will burst!' No coherent sentence, in answer to any sort of question put to her, could be extracted that morning from Mrs. Wragge" (*No Name*, Last Scene, Chapter II). As Miserrimus Dexter lapses into insanity, all distinction between the conscious and the unconscious breaks down, and his speech assumes an order that is meaningful only to the unconscious. The pattern of alternating selves in the Marillac boy, younger brother of the duelling victim of Lewis Romayne, perhaps suggests the highest potential in the use of the unconscious, which Collins, deeply involved with the principal plot in the novel, failed to develop.

Although Collins deplored the idea of stereotyped characters, as he emphasized in his essay "A Petition to the Novel-Writers," he himself developed a number of characters recognizable by type, which appeared with increasing frequency in the works of the last years. The principal reasons were technical: Collins would lose control of the individual in the class or group to which he belonged, and he wrote so much that repetition of personalities within situations was inevitable. There are, however, other causes that can be at least partially identified. The corollary of Collins' structural use of villains as the creators of conflict and the sustainers of plot is predictably a type of passive protagonist. And the kinds of narratives that he wrote—ones concerned with the ambiguities of appearance and the technicalities of the law as well as with crime and mystery—produced a small group of unfaithful clerks or retainers (beginning with Ulpius and Mannion in the early novels), a handful of amateur detectives in addition to Sergeant Cuff himself, a slightly larger group of dependable family lawyers, and here and there a clergyman of immediately recognizable reliability.

Fallen women constitute a fairly large group, but their individual cases are so strikingly dissimilar that they are hardly a type: Margaret Sherwin is vicious and unrepentant; Mary Grice, betrayed by circumstances as much as by her lover, suffers dreadfully; Sarah Leeson passes through a life of expiation; Mrs. Catherick rises to the respectability of the middle class if not to its morality; Magdalen Vanstone is fallen to the extent that she sells herself in marriage to a man whom she hates; Lydia Gwilt continually compounds her fall, only to die in weary confusion, caught between the evil with which she has learned to identify herself and her love for Ozias Midwinter; Mercy Merrick seeks redemption and re-entrance into the society which betrayed and then rejected her.

In the instances of illegitimate children, a far smaller group, there is a division between those whose illegitimacy is totally uncomplicated, such as Madonna and Anne Catherick, and those who discover late in youth that they are illegitimate, such as Rosamond Treverton (*The Dead Secret*) and Magdalen Vanstone, or those who are deprived of legitimacy by a legal technicality, such as Anne Sylvester (*Man and Wife*). The fact that Madonna and Anne Catherick suffer physical afflictions, deafness and amentia, suggests a concession by Collins to those of his readers who would expect retributive judgment.

Despite Madonna in the early novel and later Jicks (*Poor Miss Finch*) and Zo (*Heart and Science*), there are in Collins' world— as in George Eliot's and later in Thomas Hardy's—few children. But those who appear, in quite minor roles, are credible. The handicapped, like the insane, are sufficiently numerous to be mentioned, often contributing to the atmosphere existing at the surface of the narrative and to the ironic intellectual perspective beneath.

II *Narratives and Structure*

The primacy of character is evident in Collins' recurring use of individual narrators, frequently brought together in a rather complicated arrangement for dramatic and ironic revelation of what finally constitutes truth. *The Woman in White* and *The Moonstone*, the supreme instances of success with this method, rest firmly upon the assumption that the power for which the characters compete derives from the knowledge attained by reading records, letters, and diaries, to all of which the reader is given access.

Through the other novels there are variations upon the method of using records for the furtherance of plot. Geoffrey Delamayn reads the "Confessions" of Hester Dethridge, thereby acquiring a means of approaching escape from his marital confinement. In *The Dead Secret*, leading her blind husband into the Myrtle Room, Rosamond describes to him all that she sees, emphasizing what *he* needs for perspective; and Leonard, in turn, adds to the perspective a sensibility (expressed by his awareness of weight and sound) in which *she* cannot immediately participate. And when, moments later, Rosamond learns the circumstances of her birth, fearing that Leonard is blinded also by prejudice, she casts her revelation, somewhat incredibly, in the form of a discussion with him of the novel that she might write. And in *The Two Destinies*, the story of George and Mary takes the shape of a memoir which George has written and now thrusts upon his American friend, whom he asks to be the judge of their fitness for society. Here contrivance is most apparent, and its results are hardly credible, but they are characteristic of the difficulties in the novels that Collins wrote toward the end of his life; he frequently failed to establish credible frames for action and to maintain the distinction between the records of individual narrators and his own.

In some cases, though more frequently in the novels than in the

shorter narratives, Collins depended upon the law and its technical provisions for the substratum of his plots. The method was
generally successful, since the law imposes a kind of logic upon
those reactive to it, which can serve as the basis for much of the
cause-effect sequence in a given plot, removing it from dependence upon the coincidental and the gratuitous.

In other cases, the juxtaposition of two cultures or of two classes
constitutes the framework of a plot, with reasonable success when
the characters' actions proceed from expected responses to the demands of their own culture. Such is the case in *Antonina,* with
Roman cast against Goth; less successful as an informing principle
is the Anglo-American juxtaposition in *Hide and Seek,* though in
The Woman in White much of the action consistently develops
because of the differences between the aristocracy and the middle
class. The danger is, expectedly, caricature, the submersion of real
character in national type, occurring in the sensational *Jezebel's
Daughter,* in which the Franco-German Madame Fontaine becomes perhaps somewhat too savagely "un-English." And in *The
Black Robe* the framing conflict between Protestant and Catholic
may be saved from absurdity by the inclusion among the Catho-
lics of Arthur Penrose and of Romayne's dull but benign friends
the Lorings.

Collins never passed beyond dependence upon certain stock situations, one or two of which occur with disturbing frequency. Of
these the love-at-first-sight is an example, occurring in *Basil, No
Name,* and *Armadale.* Another is the device, used in two novels
(*Basil, No Name*), by which an engaged pair is forced to put off
the marriage by a year, in *Basil* with particularly slight justification. Both Allan Armadale and Mina Fontaine carry illusions
about their mothers, which their friends strive to preserve for
them. Dreams play a significant part in the development of a
number of plots, susceptible to interpretation upon either prophetic or rational grounds, thereby binding together the sensibilities of Collins' presumed audience with his own and preserving
the best of both worlds. Similarly, the theme of the resurrection of
the seeming dead contributes to the pleasure in sensationalism
sought by the public sensibility and to the symbolic representa-
tion of reaffirmation and psychological rebirth contemplated by
the more thoughtful in Collins' generation.

In some of the narratives, particularly the novels, certain objects are significant as a means both of motivating the action and of judging characters by the response that they make to these objects as symbols: a lute given Antonina by Vetranio, a hair-bracelet in *Hide and Seek*, the letter in the Myrtle Room, the Moonstone itself, and the color blue in *Poor Miss Finch*. Music or art becomes especially significant in a number of novels, in which one committed to a form of art is judged by the very manner of his commitment. Of the lute Antonina makes a symbol of continuing identity, of her own emotional survival in the dark house of her father. Valentine Blyth (*Hide and Seek*), most unsuccessfully an artist, turns back to life, with love and understanding for all men, and makes of it an art. Sarah Leeson's Uncle Joseph holds a place at the center of order and moral strength, marked by his music box that plays Mozart. Frederick Fairlie and Lady Lundie (*Man and Wife*) dabble in art, whereas Mrs. Gallilee (*Heart and Science*) entirely rejects it. Miserrimus Dexter can only improvise within the self-contained world in which he lives.

Collins' ambiguous handling of symbols, with a sense of probable public response to them and at the same time without private commitment, is nowhere illustrated as in his use of natural phenomena to express the mood of human events. The fog and rain at the time of Basil's wedding to Margaret, and the lightning giving "a hideously livid hue" to Mannion's face, the increasing rain as Mat Marksman and Mr. Thorpe confront each other, the intensification of the heat as Rosamond discovers the secret in the Myrtle Room—each of these adds to the larger emotional context in which characters act. Though sometimes recognized by the characters themselves, its significance is never explicitly asserted by the author, and whatever logical association is adduced to it derives from one character's interpretation or from a construction placed upon it by the reader himself. It becomes therefore an expression of the atmosphere characteristic of Collins' novels, achieved by the accumulation of details of setting and aspects of the situations in his plots, without in any way imposing a transcendent order upon them.

In the last years Collins moved more fully toward sensationalism than before, delighting for the moment a group of readers whose descendants in the twentieth century seem rarely to approach the level of minimal literature. In each instance he constructed or implied a fully rational explanation of the events producing sensation, allowing his readers to impose what construction they might upon the materials given them. In very few instances did he attain physical horror, and the direct action, the violent confrontation, in these novels is quite limited. Since on most occasions action really takes place in the minds of the characters, the mood is largely created in the imaginations of the readers, stimulated but ultimately left free to work as they will.

Wilkie Collins is supposed to have succumbed not only to bad health and the addiction to laudanum but to the urge toward social criticism. An obvious danger in using fiction for social criticism is the subordination of the elements of plot to the social purpose. Another, seen in the perspective of several generations, is that the social disorder of one age may seem trivial in the next; the twentieth century does not forgive Mercy Merrick so much as overlook her. For his social fiction, Collins has suffered on both counts. It is not accurate, however, to propose that toward the end he suddenly became a social critic, as another man might deteriorate in another way. As early as *Antonina*, Numerian comes forth to illustrate the social evils of religious fanaticism; and there is no more intense exposure of the horrors of the crass middle-class life in an industrial civilization than *Basil*. The absurdity of moral distinctions based upon wealth dominates *The Dead Secret*, and the inadequacy of the laws of inheritance and marriage is a principal theme in *The Woman in White, No Name,* and *Armadale*. The point is not that Collins succumbed in his last years to the urge to write social criticism but that he became less restrained in doing it.

Collins could hardly write anything else. His world is the world of social relations, of nineteenth-century man, deep in his industrialization and his attempts to rule himself, deprived of much of the authoritarian solace of the past. It is a world of the individual, bounded by men living together but in an alien universe. Ultimately, the social relationship, interpersonal and intersubjective, becomes all, the source of value and of fulfillment. And the writer may turn his attention to what underlies that relationship. Collins made the commitment in his works to the world he knew, and in this lay his success and his failure.

Notes and References

Chapter 1

1. See the Chronology and the Bibliography. A definitive bibliography of Wilkie Collins, yet to be done, would pose the difficulties familiar to those who study Victorian fiction, particularly because of periodical publication and reprinting of many pieces in England and the republication, authorized and pirated, in the United States. To date the most complete bibliography is R. V. Andrew's "A Wilkie Collins Check-List," *English Studies in Africa,* III (1960), 79–98—a work upon which my own dependence has been extensive.

2. See Dougald B. MacEachen, "Wilkie Collins and British Law," *Nineteenth-Century Fiction,* V (1950), 121–39.

3. For a clear account of the publication of and the reaction to *The Woman in White,* see Kenneth Robinson, *Wilkie Collins. A Biography* (London, 1951), pp. 142–49.

4. Nat Beard, "Some Recollections of Yesterday," *Temple Bar,* CII (1894), 315–39; Hall Caine, *My Story* (New York, 1909), pp. 319–35. In addition, there are, among others, the accounts by Mr. and Mrs. Bancroft, Gladys Storey, and William Winter (see Bibliography).

5. Robinson (1951); Robert Ashley, *Wilkie Collins* (New York, 1952); and Nuel Pharr Davis, *The Life of Wilkie Collins* (Urbana, 1956). Although every biographer of Collins must be forced into conjecture, Robinson and Ashley made the point when their conclusions were conjectural. Davis, writing an extremely lively book, frequently failed to make explicit the conjectural nature of what he was asserting as fact; thus, he incorporated into his narrative dialogue drawn from the novels as if it had been taken from factual sources; and he treated the *conjecturally deducible* as if it were *historically demonstrable* fact. See Francis Russell Hart, "Wilkie Collins and the Problem of Biographical Evidence," *The Victorian Newsletter,* No. 12 (Autumn 1957), pp. 18–21.

6. See George H. Ford's excellent study *Dickens and His Readers: Aspects of Novel-Criticism since 1836* (Princeton, 1955). Although this book is not directly concerned with Collins, it is essential for anyone wishing to understand the sociocultural context of the pub-

lication and reception of the work of Collins or of any other Victorian novelist attempting to maintain intellectual integrity and at the same time to appeal to the mass reading public. For similar reasons, see Richard D. Altick, *The English Common Reader. A Social History of the Mass Reading Public 1800–1900* (Chicago, 1957).

7. Cornelius Weygandt, *A Century of the English Novel* (New York, 1925), p. 70.

8. T. S. Eliot, "Wilkie Collins and Dickens," *Times Literary Supplement,* August 4, 1927, pp. 525–26 (reprinted in *Selected Essays, 1917–1932* [New York, 1947], p. 377).

9. John Forster's *Life of Charles Dickens* was first published in installments, from 1872 to 1874. In our own century it has been edited and annotated by J. W. T. Ley (London, 1928). The controversy over the degree to which Collins and Dickens were associated, and particularly over the direction of literary influence, is extensive and, in some respects, futile.

Today the consensus of responsible critical opinion holds that the influence was reciprocal, operating with varying degrees of intensity at different times. See Hesketh Pearson, *Dickens* (London, 1949), especially pp. 210–14; Arthur A. Adrian, "A Note on the Dickens-Collins Friendship," *Huntington Library Quarterly,* XVI (1953), 211–13; and Robert P. Ashley, "Wilkie Collins and the Dickensians," *The Dickensian,* XLIX (1953), 59–65.

10. See for example, Dorothy L. Sayers, ed. *The Omnibus of Crime* (New York, 1929), pp. 25–28; Malcolm Elwin, "Wilkie Collins: the Pioneer of the Thriller," *London Mercury,* XXIII (1931), 574–84; Maurice Richardson, ed. *Novels of Mystery from the Victorian Era* (London, 1945), pp. vii–xiii; Dorothy L. Sayers, "Introduction" to *The Moonstone* (New York, 1945); Edward Wagenknecht, ed. *Murder by Gaslight: Victorian Tales* (New York, 1949), *passim;* Robert P. Ashley, "Wilkie Collins and the Detective Story," *Nineteenth-Century Fiction,* VI (1951), 47–60; V. S. Pritchett, "The Roots of Detection" in *Books in General* (London, 1953), pp. 179–84; Alma Elizabeth Murch, *The Development of the Detective Novel* (London, 1958), pp. 102–14.

11. E. D. Forgues, "Études sur Le Roman Anglais. William Wilkie Collins." *Revue des Deux Mondes,* 2e Série, XII (1855), 815–48. Recognizing the assistance given his reputation at this stage in his career, Collins was not ungrateful: four years later he dedicated *The Queen of Hearts* to Forgues.

12. Algernon Swinburne, "Wilkie Collins," *The Fortnightly Review,* LII (1889), 589–99 (reprinted in *The Complete Works of Algernon Charles Swinburne,* ed. Sir Edmund Gosse and Thomas James Wise. The Bonchurch Edition [London, 1925–27], XV, 289–306).

13. Arthur Compton-Rickett, "Wilkie Collins," *The Bookman*, XLII (1912), 107–14.

14. Robert P. Ashley, "Wilkie Collins Reconsidered," *Nineteenth-Century Fiction*, IV (1950), 265–73; Bradford A. Booth, "Wilkie Collins and the Art of Fiction," *Nineteenth-Century Fiction*, VI (1951), 131–43. At least three American doctoral dissertations have been produced in our own time: James Wye Milley, "The Achievement of Wilkie Collins and his Influence on Dickens and Trollope" (Yale, 1941); Robert P. Ashley, Jr., "The Career of Wilkie Collins" (Harvard, 1948); and Dougald B. MacEachen, "Wilkie Collins: Victorian Crusader" (Cincinnati, 1948).

15. There have been various reactions to Collins' repeated use of the prefaces to his volumes as means of expressing his literary dicta. Whatever the advisability of such extraliterary devices may be, they clearly give the critic a lead into the intrinsic qualities of the works themselves. The most useful prefaces seem to be those to *Basil* (1852), *Hide and Seek* (1854), *The Woman in White* (1860), *No Name* (1862), and perhaps *Heart and Science* (1883).

16. Compton-Rickett, pp. 109–11.

17. Eliot, *Selected Essays*, p. 380.

18. Michael Sadleir, *Excursions in Victorian Bibliography* (London, 1922), p. 131.

19. *My Miscellanies* (Harper Edition), pp. 59–70.

20. Chapter IV (Peter Fenelon Collier Edition, XXVIII, 97). Since Collins' works are unevenly available, hereafter, whenever feasible, I shall indicate, within parentheses in my text, the number of the chapter in a novel from which a phrase or a passage has been taken, or, in the instances when chapters are not marked off or indicated, the name of the section or division.

21. Max Weber, *The Protestant Ethic and the Spirit of Capitalism* (New York, 1958), pp. 169–70.

22. See W. F. Galloway, Jr., "The Conservative Attitude Toward Fiction, 1770–1830," *Publications of the Modern Language Association*, LV (1940), 1041–59; J. T. Taylor, *Early Opposition to the English Novel: The Popular Reaction from 1760 to 1830* (New York, 1943).

23. For discussion of the growth of the English reading public and the situation that it engendered, see Walter C. Phillips, *Dickens, Reade, and Collins. Sensation Novelists* (New York, 1919), and Richard D. Altick.

24. Ford, p. 27

25. Reprinted in *My Miscellanies* (Harper Edition), pp. 140–41.

26. *Ibid.*, 60.

Chapter 2

1. Robinson, p. 43.
2. Davis, *passim*. One of the major themes of Mr. Davis' book, the deep and motivating hatred that Wilkie Collins had for his father, rests largely upon the supposed evidence in the novels, especially upon the identification of malign father types with William Collins. Selecting instances that support his thesis, Mr. Davis has ignored others such as Walter Hartright's description of *his* father, in the opening of *The Woman in White,* which, as we know from many available sources, could accurately describe William Collins: "My father was a drawing-master before me. His exertions had made him highly successful in his profession; and his affectionate anxiety to provide for the future of those who were dependent on his labors had impelled him, from the time of his marriage, to devote to the insuring of his life a much larger portion of his income than most men consider it necessary to set aside for that purpose. Thanks to his admirable prudence and self-denial, my mother and sister were left, after his death, as independent of the world as they had been during his lifetime."
3. *Hide and Seek* (Harper Edition), pp. 9–10.
4. An excellent discussion of *Household Words* is to be found in Edgar Johnson, *Charles Dickens. His Tragedy and Triumph* (New York, 1952), II, 701–18.
5. Davis (p. 195) has written: "The maid's secret—she had passed off her child as her mistress's—did not amount to much. Wilkie, however, kept it suspended throughout the story, and it gave the *Household Words* reader a sense of unity and progress in the episodes."

Chapter 3

1. See Johnson, II, 944 ff.
2. Robinson, p. 73.
3. Ashley, *Wilkie Collins,* p. 55.
4. See Pierce Egan, *Account of the Trial of Mr. Fauntleroy* (London, 1824); *Encyclopedia Britannica* (11th Edition).
5. Ashley, *Wilkie Collins,* p. 51.
6. Robinson (pp. 158–59) discusses this extraordinary and confusing situation. Throughout, I have depended heavily upon Robinson for information about the composition and production of Collins' plays.
7. *Ibid.,* 173–74. Ashley (*Wilkie Collins,* p. 125) records that a version of *No Name* was produced in New York, at the Fifth Avenue Theatre, from June 7 through 16, 1871, by Augustan Daly; this might well have been Reeve's adaptation.

8. Robinson (p. 199) is uncertain; Davis (pp. 247–49) denies that the French version was produced.

9. Robinson, pp. 205–10. For a useful discussion of the stage-history of Collins' plays in America, see Robert Ashley, "Wilkie Collins and the American Theatre," *Nineteenth-Century Fiction*, VIII (1954), 241–55.

10. Robinson, pp. 225–26.

11. Douglas William Jerrold (1803–57), dramatist and man of letters, is remembered for his contributions to *Punch*.

12. Clyde K. Hyder ("Wilkie Collins and *The Woman in White*," *Publications of the Modern Language Association*, LIV [1939], 298–303) points to Collins' partial source as J. Peuchet's *Mémoires tirés des Archives de la Police de Paris* (Paris, 1838).

13. Edward Fitzball (1792–1873), *Thirty-five Years of a Dramatic Author's Life* (London, 1859).

Chapter 4

1. The novel concluded in *Harper's Weekly* three weeks earlier than in *All the Year Round* because Harper and Brothers attempted anticipating the efforts of the American pirates. Although there was at this time no copyright protection for British authors in the United States, Harper's generously paid Collins £500 for the advance proofs. Obviously, as soon as the proofs of the final chapters of *The Woman in White* were in hand, Harper's prepared to publish both the final installments in the *Weekly* and the book itself, which appeared about August 15. Kenneth Robinson has remarked (p. 146): "It is significant that in Harper's first edition the copious illustrations which decorate most of the text stop short two or three chapters from the end, indicating that no time could be spared for the illustrator once the final instalment of proofs had crossed the Atlantic."

2. Robinson, p. 142.

3. The probable source of Collins' idea for the plot lay in the sensational French case during the early part of the century, in which the Marquise de Douhault attempted to prove her living identity and retrieve the property which her brother had taken from her by persuading the world of her death. See Hyder, "Wilkie Collins and *The Woman in White*."

4. Eliot, *Selected Essays*, p. 376.

5. *Loc. cit.*

6. *Ibid.*, 380.

7. Robinson, p. 195.

8. *Ibid.*, 190.

Chapter 5

1. Dorothy L. Sayers, ed. *The Omnibus of Crime*, p. 25.
2. Robinson, p. 218.
3. In addition to the biographies and critical works already cited, I have consulted, in preparing my discussion of *The Moonstone*, a number of useful essays: T. S. Eliot, "Introduction" to *The Moonstone* (Oxford, 1932); Alexander Woollcott, "Foreword" to *The Moonstone* (New York, 1943); G. F. McCleary, "A Victorian Classic," *The Fortnightly Review*, CLXVI (1946), 137–41; Charles Rycroft, "A Detective Story: Psychoanalytic Observations," *Psychoanalytic Quarterly*, XXVI (1957), 229–45; Lewis A. Lawson, "Wilkie Collins and *The Moonstone*," *The American Imago*, XX (1963), 61–79; Lauriat Lane, Jr., "Introduction" to *The Moonstone* (New York, 1965); Lucille Jones Webster, "Introduction" to *The Moonstone* (New York, 1965); Peter Wolfe, "Point of View and Characterization in Wilkie Collins' *The Moonstone*," *Forum*, IV (1965), 27–29; J. I. M. Stewart, "Introduction" to *The Moonstone* (Baltimore, 1966).
4. Dorothy L. Sayers (*The Omnibus of Crime*, p. 26) has remarked: "The figure of Sergeant Cuff is drawn with a restraint and sobriety which makes him seem a little colourless beside Holmes and Thorndyke and Carrados, but he is a very living figure." Such an observation, relying too heavily upon the appearance of the man, suppresses the fact that from the counterpoint established throughout the action between his appearance and reality emerges the strength of the literary character.
5. For discussion of the way in which the major Victorian novel reflects such serious intellectual concerns of the nineteenth century, see my own book *The World of the Victorian Novel* (New York and South Brunswick, New Jersey, 1967).
6. Several critics have deplored aspects of Betteredge's narrative, especially its apparent tedium and its pretensions to learning. Dorothy L. Sayers (*The Omnibus of Crime*, p. 25) has remarked: "Betteredge's narrative is not at all the kind of thing that a butler would be likely to write." Such a judgment does not take into consideration the degree to which the old man would have been able to read superficially in standard works and to impress the results of his reading upon his occupational, and probably intellectual, inferiors.
7. See Ian Watt, "*Robinson Crusoe* as Myth," *Essays in Criticism*, I (1951), 95–119 (reprinted in *Eighteenth-Century English Literature. Modern Essays in Criticism*, ed. James L. Clifford [New York, 1959], pp. 158–79).
8. The idea of the *unconscious* has been familiar to European thinkers since approximately 1750. Obviously, it was during the nine-

teenth century that the transition was made between what Coleridge regarded as a higher, creative faculty and the *subconscious* of Sigmund Freud. See Lancelot Law Whyte, *The Unconscious before Freud* (New York, 1960). The importance of Wilkie Collins' contribution to this transition, the degree to which he was obviously aware of the implications of the notions about the unconscious, has never been sufficiently appraised.

9. Robinson, p. 239.

Chapter 6

1. Robinson, p. 260.
2. *Complete Works*, XV, 300.
3. Robinson, p. 291.
4. *Complete Works*, XV, 300.
5. Anon., "Bodily Illness as a Mental Stimulant," *The Cornhill Magazine*, XXXIX (1879), 412–26.
6. See Dougald B. MacEachen, "Wilkie Collins' *Heart and Science* and the Vivisection Controversy," *The Victorian Newsletter*, No. 29 (Spring 1966), 22–25.
7. Morse Peckham, "Darwinism and Darwinisticism," *Victorian Studies*, III (1959), 19–40.
8. See Robert Ashley, "Wilkie Collins and a Vermont Murder Trial," *New England Quarterly*, XXI (1948), 368–73.
9. *Ibid.*, 373.
10. Eliot, *Selected Essays*, p. 380.

Chapter 7

1. See J. Hillis Miller, *Charles Dickens. The World of His Novels* (Cambridge, Massachusetts, 1959).
2. The term *negative absolutism* was suggested to me by Professor Robert L. Mortenson. In *The World of the Victorian Novel* (pp. 133–35, 465), I have discussed instances of this phenomenon depicted in some of the major English novels of the latter half of the nineteenth century.
3. Davis (pp. 211–12) has remarked of Collins: "Being an atheist, for example, he was debarred from all that aspect of the human drama even remotely connected with sin and salvation." While Collins himself apparently did not literally believe in sin and salvation, he internalized them in his fiction, rendering them powerful motives for human action in the social sphere.
4. *Rambles Beyond Railways* (London, 1851). Although this early work was reprinted by Bentley (1852, 1861), it was not included in the collected editions of Collins' works.
5. For a significant discussion of the literary reflection of the secu-

lar world of the nineteenth century, to which, obviously, Collins belonged, see J. Hillis Miller, *The Disappearance of God. Five Nineteenth-Century Writers* (Cambridge, Massachusetts, 1963).

Chapter 8

1. For parallel treatment of the matters discussed in the preceding
and particularly in this chapter, see especially the opening chapter of
James Wye Milley's unpublished dissertation, "The Achievement of
Wilkie Collins and his Influence on Dickens and Trollope" (Yale,
1941). Although I came to this work after I had reached my own
general conclusions and had set up areas for discussion, I found it a
significant and stimulating piece of scholarship.

Selected Bibliography

I. Books

Memoirs of the Life of William Collins, Esq., R. A. with Selections from His Journals and Correspondence. 2 vols. London: Longman, Brown, Green, and Longmans, 1848.

Antonina; or, The Fall of Rome. A Romance of the Fifth Century. 3 vols. London: Bentley, 1850.

Rambles Beyond Railways; or, Notes in Cornwall Taken A foot. London: Bentley, 1851.

Mr. Wray's Cash-Box; or, the Mask and the Mystery. A Christmas Sketch. London: Bentley, 1852.

Basil: A Story of Modern Life. 3 vols. London: Bentley, 1852.

Hide and Seek. 3 vols. London: Bentley, 1854.

After Dark. 2 vols. London: Smith & Elder, 1856. Connected by "Leaves from Leah's Diary" are six narratives, of which five were published previously in *Household Words:* "A Terribly Strange Bed" (*HW*, April 24, 1852), "A Stolen Letter" (*HW*, Christmas number for 1854, entitled *The Seven Poor Travellers*), "Sister Rose" (*HW*, April 7–28, 1855), "The Lady of Glenwith Grange" (first publication), "Gabriel's Marriage" (*HW*, April 16–23, 1853), "The Yellow Mask" (*HW*, July 7–28, 1855).

The Dead Secret. 2 vols. London: Bradbury & Evans, 1857. (First published serially, in *Household Words,* January 3–June 13, 1857.)

The Queen of Hearts. 3 vols. London: Hurst & Blackett, 1859. Within connecting narrative are ten fictional pieces previously published: "The Siege of the Black Cottage" (*Harper's New Monthly Magazine,* February 1857), "The Family Secret" (as "Uncle George; or the Family Mystery," *The National Magazine* [New York], May 1857), "The Dream-Woman" (as "The Ostler," *Household Words,* Christmas number for 1855, entitled *The Holly-Tree Inn*), "Mad Monkton" (as "The Monktons of Wincot Abbey," *Fraser's Magazine,* November–December 1855), "The Dead Hand" (*HW*,

October 10, 1857), "The Biter Bit" (as "Who is the Thief?" *The Atlantic Monthly*, April 1858), "The Parson's Scruple" (as "A New Mind," *HW*, January 1, 1859), "A Plot in Private Life" (as "A Marriage Tragedy," *Harper's New Monthly Magazine*, February 1858), "Fauntleroy" (as "A Paradoxical Experience," *HW*, November 13, 1858), "Anne Rodway" (as "The Diary of Anne Rodway," *HW*, July 19–26, 1856).

The Woman in White. 3 vols. London: Sampson Low, 1860. (First published serially, in *All the Year Round*, November 26, 1859–August 25, 1860.)

No Name. 3 vols. London: Sampson Low, 1862. (First published serially, in *All the Year Round*, March 15, 1862–January 17, 1863.)

My Miscellanies. 2 vols. London: Sampson Low, 1863. Selected and revised by Collins himself are essays previously published in *Household Words* and *All the Year Round:* "Talk-Stoppers" (*HW*, October 25, 1856), "A Journey in Search of Nothing" (*HW*, September 5, 1857), "A Queen's Revenge" (*HW*, August 15, 1857), "A Petition to the Novel-Writers" (*HW*, December 6, 1856), "Laid Up In Lodgings" (*HW*, June 7–14, 1856), "A Shockingly Rude Article" (*HW*, August 28, 1858), "The Great (Forgotten) Invasion" (*HW*, March 12, 1859), "The Unknown Public" (*HW*, August 21, 1858), "Give Us Room!" (*HW*, February 13, 1858), "Portrait of An Author, Painted by His Publisher" (*AYR*, June 18–25, 1859), "My Black Mirror" (*HW*, September 6, 1856), "Mrs. Badgery" (*HW*, September 26, 1857), "Memoirs of an Adopted Son" (*AYR*, April 20, 1861), "The Bachelor Bedroom" (*AYR*, August 6, 1859), "A Remarkable Revolution" (*HW*, August 1, 1857), "Douglas Jerrold" (*HW*, February 5, 1859), "Pray Employ Major Namby!" (*AYR*, June 4, 1859), "The Poisoned Meal" (*HW*, September 18–October 2, 1858), "My Spinsters" (*HW*, August 23, 1856), "Dramatic Grub Street" (*HW*, March 6, 1858), "To Think, or Be Thought For?" (*HW*, September 13, 1856), "Save Me from My Friends" (*HW*, January 16, 1858), "The Caldron of Oil" (*AYR*, May 11, 1861), "Bold Words by A Bachelor" (*HW*, December 13, 1856), "Mrs. Bullwinkle" (*HW*, April 17, 1858).

Armadale. 2 vols. London: Smith & Elder, 1866. (First published serially, in *The Cornhill Magazine*, November, 1864–June, 1866.)

The Moonstone. A Romance. 3 vols. London: Tinsley, 1868. (First published serially, in *All the Year Round*, January 4–August 8, 1868.)

Man and Wife. A Novel. 3 vols. London: F. S. Ellis, 1870. (First published serially, in *Cassell's Magazine*, January–September, 1870.)

Poor Miss Finch. A Novel. 3 vols. London: Bentley, 1872. (First published serially, in *Cassell's Magazine*, October, 1871–March, 1872.)

The New Magdalen. A Novel. 2 vols. London: Bentley, 1873. (First published serially, in *Temple Bar*, January–December, 1872.)

Miss or Mrs? and Other Stories in Outline. London: Bentley, 1873. Reprinted are three pieces of fiction, though four in 1875 edition of the volume: "Miss or Mrs?" (first published, *The London Graphic Illustrated Newspaper*, December 13, 1871); "Blow Up with the Brig!" (as "The Ghost in the Cupboard Room," *AYR*, Christmas number for 1859, entitled *The Haunted House*); "The Fatal Cradle" (as "Picking Up Waifs at Sea," *AYR*, Christmas number for 1861, entitled *Tom Tiddler's Ground*); "A Mad Marriage" (as "A Fatal Fortune," *AYR*, October 17–24, 1874).

The Frozen Deep and Other Tales. 2 vols. London: Bentley, 1874. Republished are three narratives: "The Frozen Deep" (adapted from the play, first published serially, in *Temple Bar*, August–October, 1874), "The Dream Woman" (revised for public readings in America: see *Queen of Hearts*, above), "John Jago's Ghost" (first published serially, in *The Home Journal* [London], December, 1873–February, 1874).

The Law and the Lady. 3 vols. London: Chatto & Windus, 1875. (First published serially, in *The London Graphic Illustrated Newspaper*, early 1875 [files not available].)

The Two Destinies. A Romance. 2 vols. London: Chatto & Windus, 1876. (First published serially in *Temple Bar*, January–August, 1876.)

The Haunted Hotel, a Mystery of Modern Venice; to which is added My Lady's Money, 2 vols. London: Chatto & Windus, 1879. Each narrative was previously published: *The Haunted Hotel* in *Belgravia Magazine*, June–November, 1878; *My Lady's Money* in *The London Illustrated News*, December, 1877.

A Rogue's Life. From His Birth to His Marriage. London: Bentley, 1879. (First published serially, in *Household Words*, March 1–29, 1856.)

The Fallen Leaves—First Series. 3 vols. London: Chatto & Windus, 1879. (First published serially, in *The World*, January 1–July 23, 1879.)

Jezebel's Daughter. 3 vols. London: Chatto & Windus, 1880. (First published serially, in *The Bolton Weekly Journal* and other syndicated newspapers during 1879 [files not available].)

The Black Robe. 3 vols. London: Chatto & Windus, 1881. (First published serially, in *The Canadian Monthly,* November, 1880–June, 1881.)

Heart and Science. A Story of the Present Time. 3 vols. London: Chatto & Windus, 1883. (First published serially, in *Belgravia Magazine,* August, 1882–June, 1883.)

I Say No. 3 vols. London: Chatto & Windus, 1884. (First published serially, in *Harper's Weekly,* December 22, 1883–July 12, 1884.)

The Evil Genius. A Dramatic Story. 3 vols. London: Chatto & Windus, 1886. (First published serially, in *The Leigh Journal and Times,* December 11, 1885–May 11, 1886.)

The Guilty River. A Story. Bristol: Arrowsmith, 1886.

Little Novels. 3 vols. London: Chatto & Windus, 1887. Reprinted are fourteen stories: "Mrs. Zant and the Ghost" (first published as "The Ghost's Touch," *Harper's Weekly,* October 23, 1885), "Miss Morris and the Stranger" (as "How I Married Him," *The Spirit of the Times,* December 24, 1881), "Mr. Cosway and the Landlady" (as "Your Money or Your Life," *The People's Library,* December 17, 1881), "Mr. Medhurst and the Princess" (as "Royal Love," *Longman's Magazine,* Christmas 1884), "Mr. Lismore and the Widow" (as "She Loves and Lies," *The Spirit of the Times,* December 22, 1883), "Miss Jéromette and the Clergyman" (as "The Clergyman's Confession," *The Canadian Monthly,* August–September, 1875), "Miss Mina and the Groom" (as "A Shocking Story," *The International Review* [New York], November 2, 1878), "Mr. Lepel and the Housekeeper" (as "The Girl at the Gate," *The Spirit of the Times,* December 6, 1884), "Mr. Captain and the Nymph" (as "The Captain's Last Love," *The Spirit of the Times,* December 23, 1876), "Mr. Marmaduke and the Minister" (as "The Mystery of Marmaduke," *The Spirit of the Times,* December 28, 1878), "Mr. Percy and the Prophet" (as "Percy and the Prophet," *All the Year Round,* July 2, 1877), "Miss Bertha and the Yankee" (as "The Duel in Herne Wood," *The Spirit of the Times,* December 22, 1877), "Miss Dulane and My Lord" (as "An Old Maid's Husband," *The Spirit of the Times,* December 25, 1886), "Mr. Policeman and the Cook" (as "Who Killed Zebedee?" *The Seaside Library,* January 26, 1881).

The Legacy of Cain. 3 vols. London: Chatto & Windus, 1889.

Blind Love. (Completed by Walter Besant) 3 vols. London: Chatto & Windus, 1890. (First published serially, in *The Illustrated London News,* July–December, 1889.)

The Lazy Tour of Two Idle Apprentices and Other Stories. (In collaboration with Charles Dickens) Reprinted are three pieces: "The Lazy Tour of Two Idle Apprentices" (*Household Words,*

October 3–31, 1857), "No Thoroughfare" (*All the Year Round*, Christmas number for 1867), "The Perils of Certain English Prisoners (*HW*, Christmas number for 1857).

II. Uncollected Pieces

"The Last Stage Coachman," *Illuminated Magazine* (August, 1843).
"The Twin Sisters," *Bentley's Miscellany* (March, 1851).
"A Passage in the Life of Perugino Potts," *Bentley's Miscellany* (February, 1852).
"The Cruise of the Tom-Tit," *Household Words* (December 22, 1855).
"The National Gallery and the Old Masters," *HW* (October 25, 1856).
The Wreck of the Golden Mary (in collaboration with Charles Dickens), *HW* (Christmas number for 1856).
"A Fair Penitent," *HW* (July 18, 1857).
"The Yellow Tiger," *HW* (August 8, 1857).
"The Debtor's Best Friend," *HW* (September 19, 1857).
"A Deep Design on Society," *HW* (January 2, 1858).
"The Little Huguenot," *HW* (January 9, 1858).
"Thanks to Dr. Livingstone," *HW* (January 23, 1858).
"Strike," *HW* (February 6, 1858).
"A Sermon for Sepoys," *HW* (February 27, 1858).
"A Shy Scheme," *HW* (March 20, 1858).
"Awful Warning to Bachelors," *HW* (March 27, 1858).
"Sea Breezes with a London Smack," *HW* (September 4, 1858).
"Highly Proper!" *HW* (October 2, 1858).
"A Clause for the New Reform Bill" (in collaboration with Charles Dickens), *HW* (October 9, 1858).
"Doctor Dulcamara, M.P." (in collaboration with Charles Dickens), *HW* (December 18, 1858).
A House to Let (in collaboration with Charles Dickens), *HW* (Christmas number for 1858).
"Pity a Poor Prince," *HW* (January 15, 1859).
"Burns Viewed as a Hat-Peg," *HW* (February 12, 1859).
"A Column to Burns," *HW* (February 26, 1859).
"A Breach of British Privilege," *HW* (March 19, 1859).
"Sure To Be Healthy, Wealthy, and Wise," *All the Year Round* (April 30, 1859).
"A Dramatic Author," *HW* (May 28, 1859).
"The Royal Academy in Bed," *AYR* (May 28, 1859).
"New View of Society," *AYR* (August 20, 1859).
"Cooks at College," *AYR* (October 29, 1859).
"My Boys," *AYR* (January 28, 1860).
"My Girls," *AYR* (February 11, 1860).
"Boxing Day," *AYR* (December 22, 1860).

A *Message from the Sea* (in collaboration with Charles Dickens),
     AYR (Christmas number for 1860).
"A Night in the Jungle," *AYR* (August 3, 1861).
"An Unreported Speech," *AYR* (November 16, 1861).
"A Trial at Toulouse," *AYR* (February 15, 1862).
"Suggestions from a Maniac," *AYR* (February 13, 1864).
"To Let," *AYR* (June 18, 1864).
"Going into Housekeeping," *AYR* (July 8, 1865).
"The Devil's Spectacles," *The Spirit of the Times* (December 20,
     1879).
"Considerations on the Copyright Question. Addressed to an American
     Friend," *The International Review* (New York), (June, 1880).
"Fie! Fie! or the Fair Physician," *The Spirit of the Times* and *The
     Pictorial World Christmas Supplement* (December 23, 1882).
"The Poetry Did It: An Event in the Life of Major Evergreen," *The
     Spirit of the Times* (December 26, 1885).
"Victims of Circumstances, Discovered in Records of Old Trials,"
     Youth's Companion (August 19, 1886).
"The First Officer's Confession," *The Spirit of the Times* (December
     24, 1887).
"Reminiscences of a Story-Teller," *The Universal Review* (May–
     August, 1888).

SECONDARY SOURCES

I. Bibliographical Lists and Descriptions
Andrew, R. V. "A Wilkie Collins Check-List," *English Studies in
     Africa*, III (1960), 79–98. Most extensive list yet made.
Ashley, Robert P. "The Wilkie Collins Collection," *The Princeton
     University Library Chronicle*, XVII (1956), 81–84. Describes
     the Collins materials in the Morris L. Parrish Collection of Vic-
     torian Novelists.
———. "Wilkie Collins." *Victorian Fiction. A Guide to Research.* ed.
     Lionel Stevenson. Cambridge: Harvard University Press, 1964.
     Discussion of the major biographical, bibliographical, and critical
     works on Collins.
Bateson, F. W., ed. *The Cambridge Bibliography of English Literature.*
     4 vols. Cambridge, England: The University Press, 1941; Supple-
     ment, 1957. The later article, by Dorothy L. Sayers, is useful in
     its listing of the bulk of important work; but it is sometimes in-
     accurate in detail.
Cordasco, Francesco, and Kenneth W. Scott. *Wilkie Collins and*

Charles Reade: A Bibliography of Critical Notices and Studies.
Brooklyn: Long Island University Press, 1949. An annotated
bibliography in pamphlet form.

Parrish, M. L. *Wilkie Collins and Charles Reade: First Editions (with
a Few Exceptions) in the Library at Dormy House, Pine Valley,
New Jersey.* London: Privately printed, 1940. Now supplemented
by other bibliographies, this remains invaluable to students of
Collins.

Sadleir, Michael. "Wilkie Collins, 1824–1889." *Excursions in Victorian
Bibliography.* London: Chaundy & Cox, 1922. An early list, with
significant description of the first editions of Collins' works.

II. Correspondence

Letters of Charles Dickens to Wilkie Collins. Ed. Laurence Hutton.
New York: Harper and Brothers, 1892. Primarily letters of ap-
pointment and business between close friends who would today
convey such information by telephone. Unfortunately, the situation of Collins' available correspondence is such that scholars can
derive from it little information and but slightly more hope for
improvement. Collins' letters, presumably still in private hands,
were often partially quoted by those who wrote recollections of
him.

"Some Unpublished Letters of Wilkie Collins," *Bookman* (American
edition), XXXVII (1913), 67–71. Seven letters from Collins to the
American poet Paul Hamilton Hayne, dealing partly with literary
matters but largely with Collins' deteriorating health.

III. Biographical and Critical Discussions

Adrian, Arthur A. "A Note on the Dickens-Collins Friendship," *Huntington Library Quarterly,* XVI (1953), 211–13. Suggests a possible reason for the estrangement.

Ashley, Robert. *Wilkie Collins.* New York: Roy Publishers, 1952.
Eminently useful, a primarily critical study though within a biographical context.

———. "Wilkie Collins and the American Theatre," *Nineteenth-Century Fiction,* VIII (1954), 241–55. A stage-history.

———. "Wilkie Collins and the Detective Story," *Nineteenth-Century
Fiction,* VI (1951), 47–60. Collins' contribution.

———. "Wilkie Collins and the Dickensians," *The Dickensian,* XLIX
(1953), 59–65. Objects to the mistreatment of Collins by certain
Dickens biographers, such as John Forster, Percy Fitzgerald, and
J. W. T. Ley, who seemed to have diminished the one writer in
order to exalt the other.

————. "Wilkie Collins and a Vermont Murder Trial," *New England Quarterly*, XXI (1948), 368–73. The historical basis for Collins' story "John Jago's Ghost" (or "The Dead Alive").

————. "Wilkie Collins's First Short Story," *More Books*, XXIII (1948), 105–6. The story "The Twin Sisters" (1851) has the characteristics of his later and best work.

————. "Wilkie Collins Reconsidered," *Nineteenth-Century Fiction*, IV (1950), 265–73. Collins' decline with the critics rather than with the reading public; his two principal talents lay in the creation of atmosphere and of complex and ingenious plots.

Beard, Nathaniel. "Some Recollections of Yesterday," *Temple Bar*, CII (1894), 315–39. The son of Collins' physician and dear friend, Frank Beard, recalls Collins as a member of the family circle. One of the more valuable of the many personal recollections of Collins.

Booth, Bradford A. "Wilkie Collins and the Art of Fiction," *Nineteenth-Century Fiction*, VI (1951), 131–43. In the revival of interest in Collins, an early and influential study.

Caine, Hall. *My Story*. New York: D. Appleton, 1909. Knowing Collins in his later years, Caine devotes a chapter to a warm and sympathetic picture of the novelist.

Compton-Rickett, Arthur. "Wilkie Collins," *Bookman* (London), XLII (1912), 107–14. An extensive critical article; still useful today.

Corrigan, Beatrice. "Antonio Fogazzaro and Wilkie Collins," *Comparative Literature*, XIII (1961), 39–51. Collins' influence upon Fogazzaro.

Davis, Earle. "Charles Dickens and Wilkie Collins," *The Municipal University of Wichita Bulletin*, XX (1945), 3–26. Concerned primarily with the nature and degree of Collins' influence upon Dickens.

————. *The Flint and the Flame: The Artistry of Charles Dickens*. Columbia: University of Missouri Press, 1963. Chapter X, "The Collins Myth," contains ideas of the earlier article; but the treatment of both Collins and Dickens is less sympathetic.

Davis, Nuel Pharr. *The Life of Wilkie Collins*. Urbana: University of Illinois Press, 1956. Presenting much new information, this book is seriously weakened by the conjectural use of seemingly autobiographical portions of the novels, in large measure to support several thematic assumptions.

De la Mare, Walter. "The Early Novels of Wilkie Collins." *The Eighteen Sixties. Essays by Fellows of the Royal Society of Literature*. Ed. John Drinkwater. Cambridge: The University Press, 1932. An appreciation of Collins' early work, still of interest today.

Eliot, T. S. "Wilkie Collins and Dickens," (London) *Times Literary Supplement*, August 4, 1927, pp. 525–26. An important critical article, stressing the melodramatic elements in Collins and their significance, this was reprinted in *Selected Essays, 1917–1932* (New York: Harcourt, Brace, 1947). The article also became the basis for the introduction to *The Moonstone*, which Eliot wrote for the Oxford University Press publication in 1928.

Ellis, S. M. *Wilkie Collins, Le Fanu, and Others*. London: Constable, 1931. With a long opening chapter concerned with Collins, this represents an early serious treatment, which remains both just and significant.

Elwin, Malcolm. *Victorian Wallflowers*. London: Jonathan Cape, 1934. An early instance of renewed interest in Collins' work, the sympathetic chapter entitled "Wallflower the Sixth: Wilkie Collins" is a later form of the essay "Wilkie Collins: the Pioneer of the Thriller," *London Mercury*, XXIII (1931), 574–84.

Fielding, K. J. "Dickens and Wilkie Collins. A Reply. *The Dickensian*, XLIX (1953), 130–36. Proposes the independence of Collins and Dickens from each other.

Forgues, E. D. "Études sur Le Roman Anglais. William Wilkie Collins," *Revue des Deux Mondes*, 2e Série, XII (1855), 815–48. Obviously concerned with the early work and written by the translator of many of Collins' works into French, this article is probably the first significant criticism of Collins as a novelist.

Forster, John. *The Life of Charles Dickens*. Ed. J. W. T. Ley. London: Cecil Palmer, 1928. The first major biography of Dickens, this unjustly ignores Collins' place in Dickens' life; the pattern is followed by Percy Fitzgerald, *Memories of Charles Dickens* (Bristol: Arrowsmith, 1913), and J. W. T. Ley, *The Dickens Circle: A Narrative of the Novelist's Friendships* (London: Chapman & Hall, 1918).

Hart, Francis Russell. "Wilkie Collins and the Problem of Biographical Evidence," *The Victorian Newsletter*, No. 12 (Autumn 1957), pp. 18–21. A review-article concerned with Nuel Pharr Davis' *The Life of Wilkie Collins* and the question of the validity of the conjectural method used.

Hyder, Clyde K. "Wilkie Collins and *The Woman in White*," *Publications of the Modern Language Association*, LIV (1939), 297–303. A significant article, concerned with the biographical background of the novel and its sources.

———. "Wilkie Collins in America," *University of Kansas Humanistic Studies*, VI (1940), 50–58. An important contribution in an area about which much is still to be learned.

Johnson, Edgar, *Charles Dickens. His Tragedy and Triumph*. 2 vols.

New York: Simon & Schuster, 1952. An excellent biography, this
reveals Collins, through its many references to him, as a whole
and sympathetic human being and as Dickens' close friend.

Lawson, Lewis A. "Wilkie Collins and *The Moonstone,*" *American
Imago,* XX (1963), 61–79. Concerned primarily with the sexual
symbolism of *The Moonstone.*

Lehmann, R. C. *Charles Dickens as Editor.* New York: Sturgis &
Walton, 1912. Establishes the close relation between Collins and
Dickens.

Ley, J. W. T. "Wilkie Collins' Influence upon Dickens," *The Dickensian,* XX (1924), 65–69. Regards the influence as unfortunate.

MacEachen, Dougald B. "Wilkie Collins and British Law," *Nineteenth-
Century Fiction,* V (1950), 121–39. Collins' concern with the
inequities of the Law.

————. "Wilkie Collins' *Heart and Science* and the Vivisection Controversy," *The Victorian Newsletter,* No. 29 (Spring 1966), pp.
22–25. Discussion of the controversy raging during the latter
half of the century and of Collins' character Dr. Benjulia as a
monstrous representative of the vivisectionists.

McCleary, G. F. "A Victorian Classic," *The Fortnightly Review,*
CLXVI (1946), 137–41. *The Moonstone* as the first detective
novel.

Milley, H. J. W. "*The Eustace Diamonds* and *The Moonstone,*" *Studies
in Philology,* XXXVI (1939), 651–63. The proposal that Trollope's novel is a satiric recapitulation of Collins'.

————. "Wilkie Collins and *A Tale of Two Cities,*" *Modern Language
Review,* XXXIV (1939), 525–34. The novelette *Sister Rose,*
rather than Carlyle's *French Revolution,* influential upon Dickens'
choice of the background for his own novel.

Pearson, Hesketh. *Dickens, His Character, Comedy, and Career.* New
York: Harper, 1949. Preceding Edgar Johnson's biography by
three years, this one was perhaps the first to put the Collins-
Dickens relationship into perspective.

Phillips, Walter C. *Dickens, Reade, and Collins, Sensation Novelists.
A Study in the Conditions and Theories of Novel Writing in
Victorian England.* New York: Columbia University Press, 1919.
Concerned with the development of the common reading public
and of the sensation novel.

Pritchett, V. S. "The Roots of Detection." *Books in General.* London:
Chatto & Windus, 1953. Discusses Collins' place in the development of detective fiction.

Reeve, Wybert. "Recollections of Wilkie Collins," *Chambers' Journal,*
Sixth Series, IX (1905–6), 458–61. Some interesting anecdotes,
particularly about Collins' American visit.

Robinson, Kenneth. *Wilkie Collins. A Biography.* London: The Bodley Head, 1951. The first biography; an admirable piece of work, it presents Collins in full perspective.

Rycroft, Charles. "A Detective Story: Psychoanalytic Observations," *Psychoanalytic Quarterly,* XXVI (1957), 229–45. Treats with *Basil* and *The Moonstone.*

Sayers, Dorothy L., ed. *The Omnibus of Crime.* New York: Harcourt, Brace, 1929. A significant evaluation of Collins as a detective novelist: *The Moonstone* a masterpiece which has never been excelled.

Swinburne, Algernon Charles. "Wilkie Collins," *The Fortnightly Review,* LII (1889), 589–99. The most influential of the literary obituaries, it is still of major interest and importance. Reprinted in *The Complete Works of Algernon Charles Swinburne,* ed. Sir Edmund Gosse and Thomas James Wise. The Bonchurch Edition (London: Heinemann, 1925–27), XV, 289–306.

Waugh, Arthur. "Wilkie Collins and His Mantle," *The Academy and Literature,* LXII (1902), 364–65. Despite Collins' later failures, he has had no true successor in his best work.

Winter, William. *Old Friends. Being Literary Recollections of Other Days.* New York: Moffat, Yard, 1909. A chapter devoted to Collins, in which he is described fully and praised warmly by an old friend.

Wolfe, Peter. "Point of View and Characterization in Wilkie Collins' *The Moonstone,*" *Forum* (Houston), IV (1965), 27–29.

Index

All The Year Round, 40, 51, 52, 54, 56

Arnold, Matthew, 114, 115

Ashley, Robert P., 18

Balzac, Honoré de, 55

Beard, Nathaniel, 16

Bernard, W. B., 51

Besant, Walter, 15, 18, 21, 108

Booth, Bradford, 18

Brontë, Emily, *Wuthering Heights,* 102

Browning, Robert, 59; "Fra Lippo Lippi," 27; *The Ring and the Book,* 17

Bulwer Lytton, Edward, 29, 41

Byron, George Gordon, 59

Caine, Hall, 16

Carlyle, Thomas, *Sartor Resartus,* 115

Coleridge, Samuel Taylor, 25

Collins, Charles, 27

Collins, William Wilkie, decline as a literary artist, 20–21, 85, 92–93; influence of father, 27–28, 138; man of his own times, 25–26, 113–119; method and characteristics of work (characters and types), 127–131 (detection), 16–17, 35, 48, 77, 78–79, 85, 99 (epistolary method), 31, 48 (fiction of social purpose), 17–18, 46, 49, 66, 85–86, 134 (narrative and structure), 131–134 (religion), 124–126, 141 (sensationalism and the sensation novel), 30, 103, 110–111, 133–134 (two sensibilities), 21–26, 34,

36, 39, 45, 64–66, 71, 76, 79 (villainy), 119–126; popular novelist, 22–25; reputation, 15–21

WRITINGS OF:

Major canon:
A Rogue's Life, 46–47, 145; *After Dark,* 40, 48, 49, 143 (see Collected Pieces); *Antonina,* 15, 23, 29–31, 41–42, 115, 118, 123, 124, 129, 130, 132, 133, 134, 143; *Armadale,* 45, 51, 59, 71–76, 86, 92, 94, 112, 116, 118, 119, 123, 131, 132, 134, 144; *Basil,* 25, 31–34, 35, 41–42, 50, 94, 115–116, 118, 121, 123, 124, 130, 132, 133, 134, 137, 143; *The Black Robe,* 92, 103–104, 118, 122, 125, 126, 129, 132, 146; *Blind Love* (completed by Walter Besant), 15, 18, 20, 92, 108, 121, 146; *The Dead Secret,* 36–39, 115, 116, 117, 118, 128, 130, 131, 133, 134, 138, 143; *The Evil Genius,* 106, 146; *The Fallen Leaves,* 23, 102, 145; *The Frozen Deep and Other Tales,* 145 (see Collected Pieces); *The Guilty River,* 93, 146; *The Haunted Hotel, a Mystery of Modern Venice; to which is added My Lady's Money,* 145; (*Haunted Hotel*), 110–111, 118, 121 (*My Lady's Money*), 17, 93; *Heart and Science,* 104–105, 121, 124, 131, 133, 137, 146; *Hide and Seek,* 17, 34–36, 116, 117, 118, 119,

123, 124, 130, 132, 133, 137, 143; "*I Say No.*", 17, 104–105, 117, 146; *Jezebel's Daughter,* 17, 51, 92, 102–103, 118, 122, 132, 145; *The Law and the Lady,* 17, 92, 99–102, 114, 116, 117, 118, 121, 122, 123, 127, 129, 133, 145; *The Lazy Tour of Two Idle Apprentices and Other Stories,* 146–147 (*see* Collected Pieces); *The Legacy of Cain;* 20, 26, 106–108, 114, 125, 127, 146; *Little Novels,* 112, 146 (*see* Collected Pieces); *Man and Wife,* 40, 85–91, 92, 94, 116, 118, 124, 127, 128, 130, 131, 133, 144–145; *Memoirs of the Life of William Collins,* 27–29, 143; *Miss or Mrs?* *and Other Stories in Outline,* 145 (*see* Collected Pieces); *Mr. Wray's Cash-Box,* 41, 124–125, 143; *The Moonstone,* 16, 20, 31, 77–85, 92, 93, 102, 116, 118, 120–122, 124, 129, 130, 131, 133, 140, 144; *My Miscellanies,* 52, 54, 55, 144 (*see* Collected Pieces); *The New Magdalen,* 23, 92, 97–99, 116, 119, 123, 125, 130, 134, 145; *No Name,* 46, 66–71, 92, 118, 119, 121– 122, 123, 129–130, 132, 134, 137, 144; *Poor Miss Finch,* 20, 92, 93–96, 117, 119, 120, 123, 124, 125, 127, 128, 131, 133, 145; *The Queen of Hearts,* 40, 50, 143 (*see* Collected Pieces); *Rambles Beyond Railways,* 125, 143; *The Two Destinies,* 102, 131, 145; *The Woman in White,* 15, 19, 31, 40, 56–66, 72, 76, 77, 92, 93, 102, 111, 116, 117, 121, 123, 124, 127, 128, 130, 131, 132, 134, 135, 137, 138, 139, 144

PLAYS:

A Court Duel, 50; *A Message from the Sea,* 51; *Armadale,* 51;

Black and White, 52; *The Evil Genius,* 112; *The Frozen Deep,* 50–51, 108–109, 118; *The Lighthouse,* 50; *Man and Wife,* 112; *Miss Gwilt,* 51, 112; *The Moonstone,* 112; *The New Magdalen,* 112; *No Name,* 51, 138; *No Thoroughfare,* 51; *Rank and Riches,* 112; *The Red Vial,* 51; *The Woman in White,* 112

THE COLLECTED PIECES:

"A Journey in Search of Nothing," 54, 144; "A Mad Marriage" ("The Fatal Fortune"), 111, 145; "A Marriage Tragedy" ("A Plot in Private Life"), 17, 47, 144; "A New Mind" ("The Parson's Scruple"), 49, 124, 144; "A Paradoxical Experience" (Fauntleroy"), 49, 144; "A Petition to the Novel-Writers," 20, 24, 55, 129–130, 144; "A Plot in Private Life" ("A Marriage Tragedy"), 17, 47, 144; "A Queen's Revenge," 55, 144; "A Remarkable Revolution," 55, 144; "A Shocking Story" ("Miss Mina and the Groom"), 111, 146; "A Shockingly Rude Article," 144; "A Stolen Letter," 47, 143; "A Terribly Strange Bed," 40, 47, 49, 143; "An Old Maid's Husband" ("Miss Dulane and My Lord"), 146; "Anne Rodway" ("The Diary of Anne Rodway"), 17, 48, 144; "The Bachelor Bedroom," 144; "The Biter Bit" ("Who is the Thief?"), 17, 48– 49, 144; "Blow Up with the Brig" ("The Ghost in the Cupboard Room"), 145; "Bold Words by a Bachelor," 53, 144; "The Caldron of Oil," 54, 144; "The Captain's Last Love" (Mr. Captain and the Nymph"), 146; "The Clergyman's Confession"

("Miss Jéromette and the Clergyman"), 146; "The Dead Alive" (*John Jago's Ghost*), 109–110, 120, 121, 145; "The Dead Hand," 48, 49, 109, 143; "The Diary of Anne Rodway" ("Anne Rodway"), 17, 48, 144; "Douglas Jerrold," 52, 144; "Dramatic Grub Street. Explored in Two Letters," 55, 144; *The Dream-Woman* ("The Ostler"), 45–46, 113, 143, 145; "The Duel in Herne Wood" ("Miss Bertha and the Yankee"), 146; "The Family Secret" ("Uncle George, or the Family Mystery"), 48, 143; "The Fatal Cradle" ("Picking up Waifs at Sea"), 145; "The Fatal Fortune" ("A Mad Marriage"), 111, 145; "The Frozen Deep," 108–109, 118, 145; "Fauntleroy" ("A Paradoxical Experience"), 49, 144; *Gabriel's Marriage*, 41–42, 50, 93, 116, 118, 125, 143; "The Ghost in the Cupboard Room" ("Blow Up With the Brig"), 145; "The Ghost's Touch" ("Mrs. Zant and the Ghost"), 111, 146; "The Girl at the Gate" ("Mr. Lepel and the Housekeeper"), 146; "Give Us Room!" 144; "The Great (Forgotten) Invasion," 55, 144; "How I Married Him" ("Miss Morris and the Stranger"), 146; *John Jago's Ghost* ("The Dead Alive"), 109–110, 120, 121, 145; "The Lady of Glenwith Grange," 47–48, 116, 143; "Laid Up in Lodgings," 53, 144; "The Lazy Tour of Two Idle Apprentices," 146–147; *Mad Monkton* ("The Monktons of Wincot Abbey"), 43–45, 116, 143; "Memoirs of an Adopted Son," 54, 144; "Miss Bertha and the Yankee" ("The Duel in Herne Wood"),

146; "Miss Dulane and My Lord" ("An Old Maid's Husband"), 146; "Miss Jéromette and the Clergyman" ("The Clergyman's Confession"), 146; "Miss Mina and the Groom" ("A Shocking Story"), 111, 146; "Miss Morris and the Stranger" ("How I Married Him"), 146; "*Miss or Mrs.?*" 109, 123, 145; "The Monktons of Wincot Abbey" (*Mad Monkton*), 43–45, 116, 143; "Mr. Captain and the Nymph" ("The Captain's Last Love"), 146; "Mr. Cosway and the Landlady" ("Your Money or Your Life"), 146; "Mr. Lepel and the Housekeeper" ("The Girl at the Gate"), 146; "Mr. Lismore and the Widow" ("She Loves and Lies"), 146; "Mr. Marmaduke and the Minister" ("The Mystery of Marmaduke"), 146; "Mr. Medhurst and the Princess" ("Royal Love"), 146; "Mr. Percy and the Prophet" ("Percy and the Prophet"), 146; "Mr. Policeman and the Cook" ("Who Killed Zebedee?"), 146; "Mrs. Badgery," 53, 144; "Mrs. Bullwinkle," 53, 144; "Mrs. Zant and the Ghost" ("The Ghost's Touch"), 111, 146; "My Black Mirror," 53, 144; "My Spinsters," 53, 144; "The Mystery of Marmaduke" ("Mr. Marmaduke and the Minister"), 146; "No Thoroughfare," 51, 147; "The Ostler" (*The Dream-Woman*), 45–46, 113, 143, 145; "The Parson's Scruple" ("A New Mind"), 49, 124, 144; "Percy and the Prophet" ("Mr. Percy and the Prophet"), 146; "The Perils of Certain English Prisoners," 147; "Picking up Waifs at Sea" ("The Fatal

Cradle"), 145; "The Poisoned Meal," 54, 144; "Portrait of an Author, Painted by his Publisher," 55, 144; "Pray Employ Major Namby!" 53, 144; "Royal Love" ("Mr. Medhurst and the Princess"), 146; "Save Me From My Friends," 52, 144; "She Loves and Lies" ("Mr. Lismore and the Widow"), 146; "The Siege of the Black Cottage," 48, 143; *Sister Rose*, 42, 93, 109, 119, 124, 143; "Talk-Stoppers," 54, 143; "To Think or Be Thought For?" 144; "Uncle George; or the Family Mystery" ("The Family Secret"), 48, 143; "The Unknown Public," 23, 55, 144; "Who is the Thief?" ("The Biter Bit"), 17, 48–49, 144; "Who Killed Zebedee?" ("Mr. Policeman and the Cook"), 146; *The Yellow Mask*, 42–43, 103, 124, 125, 143; "Your Money or Your Life" ("Mr. Cosway and the Landlady"), 146

UNCOLLECTED PIECES:

"A Breach of British Privilege," 55, 147; "A Clause for the New Reform Bill," "A Column to Burns," 147; "A Dramatic Author," 55, 147; "A Fair Penitent," 55, 147; *A House to Let*, 147; *A Message from the Sea*, 51, 148; "A Night in the Jungle," 148; "A Passage in the Life of Perugino Potts," 147; "A Shy Scheme," 53, 147; "A Trial at Toulouse," 148; "An Unreported Speech," 54, 148; "Awful Warning to Bachelors," 53, 147; "Boxing Day," 147; "Burns Viewed as a Hat-Peg," 147; "Considerations on the Copyright Question," 148; "Cooks at College," 147; "The Cruise of the Tom-Tit," 147;

"The Debtor's Best Friend," 147; "Deep Design on Society," 147; "The Devil's Spectacles," 148; "Doctor Dulcamara, M. P.," 147; "Fie! Fie! or the Fair Physician," 148; "The First Officer's Confession," 148; "Going Into Housekeeping," 148; "Highly Proper!" 54, 147; "The Last Stage Coachman," 53–54, 147; "The Little Huguenot," 147; "My Boys," 147; "My Girls," 147; "The National Gallery and the Old Masters," 147; "New View of Society," 54, 147; "Pity a Poor Prince," 147; "The Poetry Did It: An Event in the Life of Major Evergreen," 148; "Reminiscences of a Story-Teller," 148; "The Royal Academy in Bed," 147; "Sea-Breezes with a London Smack," 54, 147; "A Sermon for Sepoys," 54, 147; "Strike," 55, 147; "Suggestions from a Maniac," 148; "Sure to be Healthy, Wealthy and Wise," 53, 147; "Thanks to Dr. Livingstone," 147; "To Let," 148; "The Twin Sisters," 147; "Victims of Circumstances, Discovered in Records of Old Trials," 148; *The Wreck of the Golden Mary*, 147; "The Yellow Tiger," 147

Collins, William, 15, 27–29; picture drawn by Wilkie, 27, 138; sabbatariansim, 28

Compton-Rickett, Arthur, 18–19

Darwin, Charles (Darwinism, Darwinian Movement), 25, 26, 106, 114; *On the Origin of Species*, 106

Defoe, Daniel, *Moll Flanders*, 78; *Robinson Crusoe*, 83–84

Dickens, Charles, 15, 16, 21, 36, 40, 41, 43, 47, 49, 50, 51, 52, 56, 116, 126, 136; *A Tale of Two*

Cities, 64; *Great Expectations,* 48; *Little Dorrit,* 34
Disraeli, Benjamin, 113
Duclos, Charles Pineau, 55

Eliot, George, 21, 90, 131; *Middlemarch,* 17; *Romola,* 90
Eliot, T. S., 16, 18, 19, 21, 57, 63, 72, 111

Fauntleroy, Henry, 49
Fechter, Charles, 52
Fielding, Henry, *Jonathan Wild the Great,* 78
Fitzball, Edward, 55
Forgues, E. D., 136; "Etudes sur Le Roman Anglias. William Wilkie Collins," 17, 136
Forster, John, 16, 136

Godwin, William, *Caleb Williams,* 78
Graves, Caroline, 16

Hardy, Thomas, 131
Household Words, 36, 37, 39, 40, 43, 46, 47, 52, 138
Huxley, Thomas Henry, 114

James, William, 126

Lewis, Matthew Gregory, *The Monk,* 42–43

Mill, John Stewart, *Autobiography,* 115

Milton, John, *Paradise Lost,* 57, 64

Newman, John Henry, *Apologia Pro Vita Sua,* 115

Plato, 96

Reeve, Wybert, 51
Régnier, François Joseph, 51
Report of the Royal Commissioners on the Laws of Marriage, 86
Richardson, Samuel, *Pamela or Virtue Rewarded,* 33
Robinson, Kenneth, 28, 72
Rudd, Martha, 16

Sadlieir, Michael, 19
Sayers, Dorothy L., 77
Scott, Sir Walter, 113
Swinburne, Algernon Charles, 17, 96, 102; "Wilkie Collins," 17

Tennyson, Alfred Lord, *In Memoriam,* 30, 114, 115
Thackeray, William Makepeace, 15; *The Memoirs of Barry Lyndon, Esq.,* 46; *Vanity Fair,* 57
Trollope, Anthony, 126

Vidocq, François-Jules, *Mémoires,* 79

Ward, Mrs. Humphrey, *Robert Elsmere,* 114
Weber, Max, 22
Weygandt, Cornelius, 16
Wordsworth, William, 25